Hope For The Weary Heart

Second Lesson Sermons
For Lent/Easter
Cycle C

Henry F. Woodruff

CSS Publishing Company, Inc., Lima, Ohio

HOPE FOR THE WEARY HEART

Library of Congress Cataloging-in-Publication Data

Woodruff Henry F.
Hope for the weary heart : second lesson sermons for Lent/Easter, cycle C / Henry F. Woodruff.
p. cm.
ISBN 0-7880-1746-2 (alk. paper)
1. Lenten sermons. 2. Easter—Sermons. 3. Sermons, American. 4. Bible, N.T.—Sermons. 5. Lectionary preaching. I. Title.
BV4277 .W67 2000
252'.62—dc21 00-035804
CIP

This book is available in the following formats, listed by ISBN:
0-7880-1746-2 Book
0-7880-1747-0 Disk
0-7880-1748-9 Sermon Prep

For more information about CSS Publishing Company resources, visit our website at www.csspub.com.

PRINTED IN U.S.A.

To the Faculty of the Department of Religion,
Texas Christian University, 1965-1969, who
fostered my faith in the God of hope

Acknowledgements

If genuine hope grows out of the experience of a life renewed, even when renewal is unexpected and undeserved, then no person is more responsible for the pages which follow than my wife Darlene. I also want to express my gratitude to my treasured colleague in ministry, Dr. Ralph E. Dessem, who encouraged me to put in writing what I have been saying; and deep thanks and appreciation are expressed to Mrs. Sandy Jones and Mrs. Sandy Ruffner, who typed the manuscript.

Table Of Contents

"Lord, I'm Coming Home"

2 Corinthians 5:20b—6:10

Like a bridge under which much water has flowed with the passage of time, the words span generations, linking them, linking heart, mind, and spirit: "Homeward bound; I wish I was homeward bound. Home, where my thoughts escape me; home, where my love lies waiting silently for me...."

Paul Simon wrote them; you and I, and everyone who has ever lived and ever *will* live, could have written them. In the final analysis none of us doubt that "home" is more than a place; it *is* an experience of togetherness and community. It is where acceptance and welcome always overcome rejection, where isolation is replaced by family (whatever the family configuration), and where alienation is transformed by reconciliation. It is where we all long to be, but seldom are. This is why Paul Simon's words could be and often are *our* words: *We* live in the midst of profound isolation and alienation, exacerbated by virtual offices, virtual relationships, virtual lives. "Homeward bound; I wish I was homeward bound...." We wish *we* were homeward bound: home, where loneliness would no longer hold our heart in bondage; home, where fractured relationships with our children and our parents, our life partners, ourselves, even our God — would know healing and wholeness again; home, where no one — especially us! — are strangers. *We* need a bridge! — not so much one to span time and generations, but a bridge to draw together our broken and alienated lives, a bridge over which we can make the journey home.

God's gracious word of hope today for our weary heart is that the bridge has been built! God did it the day Jesus died on the cross. In that powerful act of self-giving love, what we know as "grace," God extended the hand that can and will lead us home. In the midst of our alienation and isolation God not only calls us home, but God will in fact *lead* us home.

In *our* journey it is Good News worth celebrating! It is worth celebrating because we *know* we are going somewhere. The ashes of this day, this Ash Wednesday, remind us of our own inescapable mortality and bring the stark reality of it all home to us. Can we go somewhere else? Paul — not "Simon," but the one from Tarsus — says to us a resounding "Yes!" We *can* go somewhere else, somewhere other than ultimate alienation and isolation, the obliteration of our meager lives; we can go home!

It is first home to God, and thank God we can make the journey long before those ancient words "ashes to ashes, dust to dust" are read over us. We can go home today; we can go home to God. This is primary, for if our alienation and estrangement from the very Source of our lives is not overcome, we will never be at home: not with ourselves, nor with anyone else. We go there first because it is first and foremost the human condition, our condition, that longs to be healed. You and I and the whole created order have been created to be in harmony and togetherness, all parts interlocking in what Scripture calls "Shalom." Yes, "peace," but shalom is far more than the cessation of enmity or violence; it is the togetherness of true community, "home," if you will. And the first piece to lock into place is our place with God. God has intended it to be so, and our restlessness, boredom, and emptiness, our sense of alienation and estrangement, are all signs that it isn't so. It isn't, but needs to be. This is why in his plaintive plea the apostle entreats us to "be reconciled *to God*" — not to your spouse, or to your children, or to people in the work place, school, church, or anywhere else — but be reconciled *to God*. The other will come if we first come home to God.

The Good News of hope we celebrate today, regardless of how far from home we may be, is that God has made it all possible. God *has* taken the initiative. Not waiting for us to act first, God in Christ has already acted: for you and me and all the world, for all time.

The only waiting now is God waiting for us to respond, to say, "Lord, I'm coming home," and then put feet to those words.

And God waits, and waits, and wonders, "What's keeping them?" It's not that the way has not been opened to us — it has; whatever else Paul knew in his heart about what God has done, he at least knew this. Nor have we delayed our journey home because we've been confused about the direction, with no guides along the way. We have had numerous and effective guides, instruments of grace, "servants of God" as Paul calls them: persons who themselves embodied every positive aspect of ministry as Paul lifted them up, using his own life and ministry as an example. Neither has our lack of felt need blocked our path. We *know* better than this; our deep longing to be at home is real and profound. The only place left to look is within ourselves, and there — within — it is found.

Sometimes it's just too hard to believe God would want us home and welcome us when we got there; others, perhaps, but not us. No one knows our own brokenness better than we. No one knows better than we all the reasons we would have no home with God. After all, we are the ones who wandered away in the first place! We have chosen to live for ourselves, love ourselves, and isolate ourselves. This, of course, is the underlying reason to *have* an Ash Wednesday: only those who have chosen to go the wrong way need to "repent" and return to God. And those are you and I! Knowing all of this within makes it really difficult for us to believe that God would want to know *us* again and welcome us home; so we wait until we are worthy. For most of us, it will be a long wait.

Sometimes it's not only God's willingness to receive and welcome us home that is hard to accept; sometimes our reluctance to move is also because the way home itself looks too hard. We don't want to go that way, so we wait for another path; we look in other directions. It is because we have seen and heard the way in Jesus; it is the way of the cross that leads home, and this does not appeal to us. Dying to self and living to God and others does not sound like fun. Losing our lives in the wild abandon of self-giving love for others appears way too costly. Carrying the cross is a burden we'd soon as not bear. "Isn't there another way home?" we ask; or at least some fudging we can do — like die a little bit, love a little bit, carry it a little bit? We wait for the answer, guarding our steps, guarding our options; and God waits for us.

Sometimes those options and other paths we choose completely distract and sidetrack us; we become so entangled in other directions we lose our way. Sometimes we simply set other priorities ahead of going home, all the while hearing Paul quote the great prophet, entreating us that "now is the acceptable time, now is the day of salvation," with *us* saying, "Not yet; we have some other things to do first." It is not yet time to go home. Our business needs attention. *Our* agenda, whatever it is — family, school, self — needs our attention. We can always go home later, we believe; later, when life is calmer, less hectic; later, when we have more time; later. Yes, we want to go home, but only when the timing is right; and for this, we shall wait.

All the time, however, the reasons we have not uttered the words, "Lord, I'm coming home!" and put feet to them ... are within us. God has always been calling us home. God has said, "All are worthy and welcome; none are unfit to be at home with me!" God has promised us guides along the way and God's own presence when the Way *is* hard and challenging. God has proclaimed through his servant, "Behold, now is the acceptable time; behold, now is the day of salvation." God has done all of this and more, and when we are honest with ourselves and honest with God, we *know* the truth of it: we persist in our alienation because *we* persist in it! Whether it is our own sense of unworthiness, coupled with our incredulity — "It's just too good to be true!" — or it is our own reluctance to walk in the way of the cross that leads home, or it is just our procrastination, it is always *us*.

In our alienation the stark truth confronts us: We will never get home until we decide to go home. *This* is the bridge we need — not one spanning time or generations, not even the time from "Paul of New York" to "Paul of Tarsus" — but a bridge connecting our deepest longings for healing and wholeness, for togetherness and home, with our intentionality; a bridge connecting hope with reality, heart with feet. It is one bridge God cannot build, but only be there to take our hand, usher us across, and lead us home.

When we are far enough away — and maybe it is today; when the loneliness is greatest and our sense of alienation the deepest — and maybe it is now; it will happen. Surveying the fracture of our lives, in dust and ashes, the words will well up within us; not, "Homeward bound; I wish I *was* homeward bound," but rather, "Lord, I'm coming home!" With arms outstretched and a hand for us to hold, it is all God waits to hear.

Lent 1

When Seeing Blocks Believing

Romans 10:8b-13

Home builders can reveal the secret to you: what will make the floor plan and design attractive — and sell the place — are so-called "glamor bathrooms" (you know, with huge double sinks, jacuzzi bathtubs big enough to swim in, and so on), first floor master bedroom, gourmet kitchen, and an open, flowing, "great-room-with-vaulted-ceiling-and-fireplace-in-the-corner" kind of plan. It hooks people, looks like a dream come true, and greatly enhances the possibility of closing the sale.

Not on the list, not very glamorous at all, but absolutely essential is the humble closet. In spite of the fact that they are not even included in the calculations of square footage space, no home is constructed without them. There are at least two reasons for closets, one obvious, the other somewhat embarrassing. The obvious reason is that you need a place to hang your clothes, put your shoes, and store your stuff. The other reason is that you need a place where you can suddenly throw and cram stuff when company is expected on short notice, and you don't want to be embarrassed! We couldn't live without closets! Think of what it would be like if we didn't have a place to stuff all of the clutter of our lives and get it out of the way so we didn't have to look at it.

It is the truth: no home is constructed without a closet; no life is lived without them. Oh, you might not readily see them, for they're not constructed with dry wall and nails and stud; you and I might even be embarrassed to admit we have them — but we both know they are there, inside the recesses of our mind and heart, hidden away, the places where we cram and hide away all the stuff that clutters up our otherwise neat lives. Sometimes the clutter is the consequence of a bad decision, something messy we got ourselves into by making a bad choice. Sometimes it's the hurtful things we've done or said. Sometimes what we'd like to hide away are the failures of our lives, all the "should haves" and "could haves" — but "didn'ts"! And sometimes its just our self — our *real* self, as *we* know we are, and we don't really want anyone to see that. We all have that stuff lying around, reminding us of the things and moments we'd just as soon forget, reminding us of just how fragile and broken — and human — we really are. So it's good to have a place where we can shove it and not have to look at it all the time. For people of faith, however, the clutter is different, the embarrassment deeper, and the desire to hide it — and *not* look at it, not even admit it exists — is all the much greater. This stuff, this embarrassing clutter of our not-so-faithful lives, is all the unanswered questions, all the ambiguity and gnawing doubt, all of the fragility of faith which clutters up our otherwise neat lives with God.

It works like this: our lives get touched by grace, just like Paul wrote to the Romans. We hear the word of faith; it grasps and penetrates us. We find ourselves confessing with our lips and believing in our heart that through the power of love God raised Jesus from the dead, and we find *ourselves* being raised from our own dead lives. We even find ourselves trusting, believing God that our own puny lives *will* be saved, just like Paul says. God help us, we even find ourselves believing the Scripture Paul quotes from Isaiah 28:16, that no one who believes will be put to shame! We do *all* of this! And then it happens. Life happens: something terrible, totally undeserved and without explanation happens to us, or to someone we love, or perhaps to a total stranger we've only heard about or read about. A vital, promising life is cut short. A terrible, debilitating illness saps life. A disaster swoops down inexplicably upon good, caring people. It can be — and often is — a hundred different things that happen, but the end result is always the same: Faith wavers and sometimes vanishes; we have far more questions than we ever have answers; we "call upon the Lord"... and hear nothing. And so we become not only angry, but ashamed, even embarrassed about it all, ashamed and embarrassed to cry out in desperation, "It doesn't work! We call upon the Lord, but we surely don't feel saved!" What we see is not God's care for us, or for those we love, but heartache, hurt, tragedy, inexplicable suffering. And rather than enforcing and nurturing our belief, our seeing ends up blocking our believing. Our lived experience challenges the word that Paul or anyone else preaches.

We may be ashamed and embarrassed to admit it, but we know it's true: God's presence is not always apparent to us; sometimes we look, but see only ourselves and our own struggles; sometimes we reach out and grasp only emptiness. Oh, to be sure, all of this faith-business — all of this "God caring for us, sustaining us, and saving us" business — sounds good, but in the face of what we see in our lives — the stuff we'd just as soon cram into some closet and not see — it's really hard to believe. It is vital that you and I summon the honesty to admit this to ourselves, to each other, and to the God who can raise us to new life, because we will never be able to live with authenticity until we give up the illusion of blind faith. Authentic faith is not blind, but transforms what sounds good into something that really is good, transforms blind faith into living trust. You see, authentic faith never comes until we give up the illusion that everything is great and wonderful all the time, until we unpack the closet, take out that stuff we've hidden there, take it out and look at it and deal with all of its scary reality. If you and I are going to live with authentic faith, then we're going to have to resist the seductive temptation of denying the reality of fear and failure, heartache and brokenness, pain and tragedy and all the rest of our lived experience. We're going to have to give up living the illusion that life has perfect answers to all of our questions. It doesn't!

No, the challenge of faith is to see beyond what is — all of the ugliness and hurt and ambiguity we see — to look beyond, and in the clutter of our lives trust in the relationship God offers us, not in answers we don't have now and probably never will have. With eyes of faith we can see it. We can see a relationship with God that will sustain us in whatever wilderness and dried up, lifeless desert we find ourselves. We can see a relationship that will enable us to experience victory over all the demonic, self-destructive forces in our lives. With eyes of faith we can see the lie for what it is, and the truth about living for what it is. We can see the relationship that will make all the difference in our lives — yes! — but most importantly, we can see how you and I can claim this relationship with God as our own. First, by living as if God's love was the most powerful thing in the world ... because it *is*! Oh, it may not look like it. There are times when it looks like God's love is profoundly impotent. In the face of all that would tear at our lives, in the midst of a world drowning in its own brutality and violence and injustice, it is easy to look around and sell out for something else; the temptation is great. But we know the truth of it: often, what you see blocks believing!

Paul urges and invites us to look with eyes of faith, and when we do, what we see is the absolute victory of God's love, made manifest in the resurrection of Jesus. The fact of the resurrection — which *is* a fact; the living Spirit of Christ among us in the Church witnesses to the fact of it — the fact of the resurrection confirms the victory of God's love. Sure, the victory is not complete yet. The perfection of the created order has not yet come about, and we are living between the "now" and the "not yet." We know this; this is why there still is hurt and pain and tragedy and all the rest which reminds us the victory is not yet complete. But just because the victory isn't complete doesn't mean there isn't victory. God's love is the most powerful thing in the world, and when you and I begin to live like this is true — when we begin to live the truth that love triumphs — why, then, we will claim that relationship with God that will both give us life, as well as an authentic faith for living it.

The second way we claim this relationship as our own is to live as if we were God's own — because we are! You see, God's love is not only the most powerful thing in the world, but God has chosen to love us — each and every one of us — and nothing can stop or defeat that love. So it doesn't matter ultimately when hurt and heartaches claim us, or when suffering overtakes us, or when our questions go begging in the night for answers. What matters is that God has claimed us, God is with us, God loves us. And even if we go down with the ship, we are in the arms of God. It is enough. I think this is why Paul always put "salvation" or "being saved" in the future tense. The ultimate victory lies with God, even if in the present it is hard to see.

When it happens — when it is hard to see any victory, any presence of God — it is worthwhile to remember the truth of it: sometimes seeing *blocks* believing. In those moments, look, again with eyes of faith, and see the only thing we need to see, know the only thing we need to know: *God* ... loves us. When we know it, when we've claimed this living relationship because the living God has claimed us, we shall not need closets in which to hide; praise God, we can step out and live with faith and hope.

"Hold On! Your Life Is At Stake!"

Philippians 3:17—4:1

The names of the places — Treblinka, Auschwitz, Buchenwald, and all the rest — remain seared into our memory, even as those who knew the struggle in those places still carry their numbers on their arms. The struggle was the monumental battle between the desire to obliterate life and the will to survive; in the struggle it seemed that all the power was on one side. Those in control of the places called Treblinka, Auschwitz, Buchenwald, and the rest seemed to have had every bit of the power. They strung the barbed wire and manned the machine guns; they ran the showers that weren't and the ovens that were; they seemingly controlled every aspect of the miserable lives of the men, women, and children put there — people whose only crime was that they were Jewish, or homosexual, or disabled, or suffered from some other "defect" as the Nazis defined it. *They* seemed totally impotent in the face of it all.

But the most amazing thing transpired: while some passively succumbed, others would simply not give up. They were dehumanized; they were stripped of their clothes and their dignity; they were stripped from their families and brutalized. They were treated far worse than the animals in whose cattle cars they were brought to the camps, but still they held on. Why was that?

Eric Fromm, himself a survivor of the Nazi Holocaust, discovered the truth of it: what you decide to hold on to makes a difference in how long you can hold on! Fromm witnessed it every single day in the death camp where he was incarcerated; he tells some of the story in his book *The Art of Loving*. What made the difference,

Fromm observed, was the will to hold on to the capacity to love, and the refusal to let go all reason to the contrary! And there was every reason to let go: they knew their situation was hopeless; they witnessed their own husbands and wives and children brutalized and murdered in front of them. If there was ever a time, like Job's, "to curse God and die" (Job 2:9), this one was it!

Yes, but those who didn't — those who held on because they knew their very life — in every sense of the word — was at stake — they — survived! In the most profound sense, they held on to life even when it was crushed out of them. They discovered the truth of it, the truth which came to them in the crucible of unspeakable human hurt: what you hold on to — and where you stake your very life — really does make a difference: in the living, *and* the dying, and in everything between and beyond.

It can and will make a difference for us; it is the truth for us. No barbed wire surrounds us; we are only hemmed in by the circumstances of our lives. No death camp guard threatens us; it is simply boredom, emptiness, lost possibilities, and vanished dreams, our own miserable failures; *this* is what would strip life from us. This is the "in between time" for us, and in this in between time — between now and death — it really does make a difference where we stake our lives. It is the truth for us where we are: It makes a difference what we hold on to.

There are lots of possibilities, and some are easier to hold on to than others. We can hold on to the stuff around us. This is easy; it is nearby and we can see it. Lord knows, we've got enough of it around us! So when our lives are at stake we can reach out and grab the things we've accumulated, hold on to them, and try to keep life from slipping away. But we all know its true: whatever things we have, even the rags that covered the emaciated bodies of the Holocaust victims, can be stripped from us. Nothing is permanent; stuff will not enable us to hold on to life.

Sometimes we try to hold on to ourselves. You know what this is like: we just suck it up and tell ourselves, "*We* can do this! We're bright enough, good enough, capable enough in *ourselves* to do it. We don't need anything, nor anyone else; we can do it ourselves." This, too, can work for awhile — but only for awhile. And then the crushing reality of it all falls down on us, crushing the life out of us, and we are forced to face the truth of it: We are *not* sufficient in our own puny selves to hold on to life when it is disintegrating underneath us; we need something more to grasp than ourselves.

Like the survivors Eric Fromm observed, the "something more" can be each other. There *is* strength here; there is strength from living in community, in reaching out, giving and receiving love, and forging bonds of support. And yet, all communities *also* disintegrate; they, too, are impermanent. Eventually whatever community of which we are a part will disappear, and again we are left reaching, grasping, trying, to hold on for dear life.

One choice remains, the one that lies at both the beginning and the ending of life itself. It is the choice of reaching out to Christ and holding on to him. Only here can we really stake our lives, and when our lives are at stake, this is Good News to know. Few knew it better than Paul, and it was because of his own lived experience that he could lift himself up as an example and write the words of hope he penned to his close friends at Philippi. Earlier in his life Paul had centered his life elsewhere, and it had all slipped through his grasp. He was a person of piercing intellect and as well educated as anyone could be in his time; but he discovered that neither education nor sheer intelligence could sustain him when he lay blinded and helpless on the Damascus road. Paul was fiercely proud of his family's religion — his religion — even as he was proud of his ethnic heritage. None of it, however, mattered when he faced his own profound failure before God, writing those words in the seventh chapter of Romans that tear at our heart: "I don't even understand myself. The things I want to do, I cannot; and the very things I find abhorrent are the very things I do. Wretched man that I am, who will deliver me from this body of death?"(Romans 7:19ff). He had powerful friends in powerful places, but they couldn't save him either.

In his life Paul had tried it all, until he finally made the discovery that gave him life — both in the days he had, as well as in the time beyond. It was the discovery that only Christ will not fail you, and it is only by holding on to him that you can make it. I think this is why there is such passion in his words as we read them: Paul knew that all who were enemies of the Cross were enemies of life; all who would tell you to hold on to something else and stake your life on something else — whether it was tradition, or dogma, or ritual, or status, or whatever — all who pointed you elsewhere were pointing you toward destruction. This is why Paul urged his friends to "stand firm *in the Lord*," for it is only the hand of the Lord Jesus that will preserve your life when life — and its meaning, its purpose — are all at stake.

Where you and I are standing today, this is not easy. It is not easy for any of us; I know, for I've been there, been where all of us have been: watching any hope in our lives slip through our fingers, feeling the very ground on which we are standing slide out from under our feet. Oh, we're trying to hold on; we are trying it almost every challenging day of our fragile lives. Moreover, deep down inside we know Paul is right — that only by holding on to Jesus can we hold on to life. The problem — and it's a big one — is that to hold on to Jesus, you've first got to find the hand of Christ, and then find the courage not to let go. How do we do this?

I know the answer, even as Paul knew it, but you know it, too. Every Christian knows the answer about how to find the hand of Jesus and not let go, even though we often forget or think we don't know how. Jog your memory with me: When you were slipping and sliding, grasping at anything that would save your miserable life, wasn't it Christ who grasped you? You see, we don't have to search for the One who is the foundation of our life; *Christ* is searching *for us*! It is the scandal of the Gospel: God has seen fit never to give up on us, and when others were sent to reach to us, and we turned away, God sent Jesus who never turns away. Christ is always reaching, with hand outstretched, ready to grasp ours and lift us to new life. We can count on it. Christ is reaching to us, always, because this is what Christ is always about: reaching to hold and walk with us, reaching to sustain and give strength, reaching even when life is ebbing away, reaching, *always* reaching. All we have to do is reach out, and we will be found!

Then it will be easy to hold on and not let go — because we really do know the truth of it: If we're going to get anywhere in this life — or beyond it — it is the hand of Christ that will lead us.

Grasping that hand we will celebrate the truth and power of it, whether it be an unknown and threatening future we face, or even the specter of death itself staring us in the face. Our heart and spirit will sing with Thomas Dorsey's immortal words, "Precious Lord, take my hand, lead me on, let me stand, I am tired, I am weak, I am worn; through the storm, through the night, lead me on to the light: Take my hand, precious Lord, lead me home" (*United Methodist Hymnal*, No. 474).

Lent 3

Don't Look For Any Benches

1 Corinthians 10:1-13

Let your imagination run with it; it is a riddle: What are the numbers 28, fourteen, and five all about?? Does "28" suggest the number of days we endure in February, waiting for winter to leave and spring to come? Is "fourteen" the half-way mark in this month so short in days, but oh-so-long in time? And how about "five"? — What is "five" about — the number of fingers on your hand; the days in a work week for some; the number of telephone solicitations you receive between five and six o'clock in the evening?

The answer is "all of the above, and more." You know about "all of the above"; let me tell you about the "more." "Twenty-eight" is the number of marriage licenses issued during a recent two-week period, as listed in a local neighborhood newspaper. "Fourteen" is the number of those couples whose marriages have a chance of surviving more than "five" years. What makes the difference as to which group of fourteen couples make it or don't make it is complex. Emotional maturity, healthy realism about marriage, the length of the relationship, shared values — these are all important factors, and there are others.

In every well-functioning, lasting marriage there is, however, another factor that really tips the scales: There are no benches along the way of a marriage journey that lasts. What I mean by that is that there are no resting places, where you can just sit complacently, letting it all pass you by while you disengage.

Do you get weary in the journey? Well, of course you do! Maintaining a relationship of life-giving intimacy is hard work. It requires tremendous energy, and sometimes we get tired of it all and want to rest. There are times, too, when frustration with the other person depletes our energy. There are moments when the journey itself gets so rocky that we stumble, and get cut, and even bleed a bit; in those moments we'd just love to sit down and rest awhile. But, you see, to do that is to let the journey stop, and to let it stop is deadly in a relationship. This is why when you see a long-lasting, well-functioning marriage, don't look for any benches; you won't find them.

Why is it, then, that we think we'll find some in the most important relationship we will ever have, our relationship with God? Experience in other relationships notwithstanding, we do look for, and try to create, them — benches — where in our journey with our Lord and Christ we'd love to just stop and sit awhile. We do it because our feet and heart, body and soul become weary. It is hard work following Jesus; it is harder still maintaining a relationship when so much is pushing and pulling at us, draining off time and energy in all other directions. Being pushed and pulled in all kinds of directions, sometimes we look for benches because we get lost on the journey, or confused about where we're headed, and we need a place to rest and sort it all out. God has not seen fit to control our lives, as if we were robots; nor can any human being totally penetrate the mind of God; and so there are times we lose our way, make a wrong turn, get stuck in dead ends, and cannot see with clarity where we need to go. Then, we look for benches. There are times, too, when we need the rest, not because we are bone tired, not because we are confused, but because we need a respite from the struggle. It is no secret to anyone who has sought a relationship with Christ and to journey with Christ that there are all kinds of forces that would impede that journey and destroy the relationship. The values of our faith as Christians, and the Way of the One we call Lord, are antithetical to the society around us. Sometimes we just get tired of the struggle, and then a bench looks really inviting.

Most dangerous of all, however, is complacency, the complacency that can set in when we think we've got this Christ thing down. It's easy, isn't it? We go through the motions, *do* the right things, *believe* the right creeds, *mouth* the right words ... until we convince ourselves we've arrived! We've got it made! We *have* a relationship with Christ; we *are* a Christian and church member; our journey is complete — we *are* complete — it's a done deal, so we don't have to keep following. We can just sit down in style and watch it all go by.

"Go by," it will. Whatever richness we might know in our relationship with Christ, whatever depth of meaning and purpose we could discover in living, whatever renewing hope we could have that keeps us going on living will all pass us by while we sit in our complacency. Whatever else Paul was trying to teach his friends in Corinth, and teach us, surely it is this. Paul knew that not only weariness in the journey, not only assault from without can rob us of hope and block authentic living, but we can also defeat ourselves. Complacency in grace is the threat within. Knowing this, he lifted up the ancient story of God's people on their Exodus journey as instructive for us on our journey. Paul wrote that the fact that the Israelites were mere traveling companions of Moses was not enough to insure their favor with God. The fact that they participated in sacred acts that prefigured the Christian Sacraments (this business of being "baptized" by walking through the sea, and eating and drinking "supernatural" food and drink) was of no avail when it came to pleasing God. The fact that it was God who liberated them, called and claimed them as a people did not insure God's favor upon them: They still proved unfaithful and reaped the consequences of their unfaithfulness. Pointedly, Paul says, "We will, too if we sit down in our complacency!" No sacrament — not even baptism or the Lord's Supper — is a substitute for obedient following. No ethnic, nor group identity, no past performance of faithfulness — none of it! — can insure your relationship with God; for as soon as you think you've got it made — that you've arrived — then is the very moment destruction will descend upon you.

So says Paul in his chronicle of the Hebrews in the wilderness. So says the apostle to the Corinthians; and so he says to us: "These things happened to them as a warning" *for us*. There aren't any benches along the way for us! Yes, there are threats to our relationship with God and our journey with Christ which lie outside us. This is true in any relationship that is meaningful for us; every relationship, every journey has its "wilderness," its own parched land, and we do get confused and weary with it all at times. As formidable as these threats are, however, it is the threat within, the complacency of grace, that holds the most danger for us.

Far from benches to sit on, God has given us the means to meet and be victorious over the threat within. Two resources are vital for victory: the first is the realization that even our journey within the grace of God is not a completed journey; the second resource is God's own presence and power, always available to us in the journey, if we will only reach for it.

You and I will give up our search for benches when we give up the illusion that our journey with Christ and our relationship with God are complete and finished. They are not! Following is a daily challenge, one to be engaged as long as we draw breath. To be sure, God's grace for us is complete, and the life-giving act of Jesus is complete, for us and for all humanity; there is never, nor will there ever, be a time when God's grace is not for us in all of its completeness and power — but our response to such grace is never finished. This, of course, is what the "following" is all about, and it is what our relationship with God is all about. Each and every day we are "Christians under construction," unfinished products of the grace of God. Every day holds new opportunities for us to renew and deepen our relationship with God. Each and every day holds before us the challenge of following in the Way of the One we call Lord. So don't look for any benches along the way; we will not find them.

What we *will* find is God's own presence and power to sustain us in whatever weariness we might know, how ever often we fall and stumble, bleed and hurt, however much confusion would claim us — in it all, God has promised the Presence that guides and guards, that sustains and gives hope. You see, we will not need benches if we only reach to the God who is always reaching to us. Prayer is one vehicle for doing this. In prayer we acknowledge our need for God and open ourselves to God's presence which can enter our experience, giving us strength and renewed hope for the journey. Other spiritual disciplines — fasting, study, meditation and reflection, worship, and so on — are also ways in which we can reach to

God. But especially do we connect with the power and presence of God in reaching to each other. We do not journey alone, but we are connected with each other in community, and it is through the embrace and encouragement of one another, in acts of justice and mercy, and in support and caring for each other that God becomes powerfully present. You see, "incarnation" is more than a theological doctrine, but it is especially a lived experience, a gift we can both give and receive: strength and support, the very power of God when benches cannot be found, but *we* can be.

Letting your imagination run with it, consider the days which stretch before each of us. In every one of them, look for the richness a day in relationship with Christ can bring you. Look for the joy that comes from knowing you *are* loved ultimately by God, always. Look for, and find, the hope that will be yours in the journey, regardless of how weary you become. But don't waste your time — or your life — looking for any benches. You won't find them.

Lent 4

Words We Know, But God Doesn't

2 Corinthians 5:16-21

Native Texans know the place as "the hill country." Not like the high rolling plains of the Edward's Plateau of the Panhandle, nor like the dense piney woods of the southeastern border with Louisiana, and certainly not like the God-forsaken desert mountains of the Big Bend, the hill country *is* Texas. Home to both Willie Nelson and the LBJ Ranch, there the landscape is marked by rolling limestone hills, dotted with cedar and blue bonnets. There, the air is clear and fresh, and this is why the hill country is home to something else: the McDonald Observatory of the University of Texas at Austin. The observatory produces a radio program called *Star Date*; you can listen to it on National Public Radio.

Had you been listening this last week, you would have heard the news for which we've all been waiting: On its journey through the heavens, the earth was going to reach the place where its orbital path crosses the point where both the northern and southern hemispheres are equidistant from the sun, the place which comes twice a year when night and day are of equal length. At this time of year astronomers call it the spring equinox. We just know it as spring. It is that wonderful, amazing time of the year when new life happens: through the dead, brown undergrowth poke shoots of green — crocus, daffodil, and all the rest. Trees bud; grass grows; for with the warmth of the sun life returns and surges.

Even if it wasn't real, we would create it in our heart and imagination, for we cannot live without the promise of newness. If all we knew and would ever know was only bleak, cold, and ugly lifeless days, who would want to go on? So it is that "in the bleak midwinter as frosty wind made moan, when earth stood hard as iron and water like a stone" ("In The Bleak Midwinter," Christina Rosetti), we waited. And now the waiting is over. This earth we call home finally got there.

The issue, of course, is how do *we* get there. Not the earth, but us — our lives, dried up, hard as iron, stony cold, lifeless and making moan — how do we get there, to the place and time when light banishes darkness, deadness is transformed into life, and new beginnings come; how do *we* get there?

There aren't any of us here that don't want to know the answer to that question. It may be your own failures that hold you in their grip, all the ways and times you've messed up, and they just won't let go of you — and you won't or can't let go of them. It may be your disappointments and lost, wasted opportunities — all the things you could have done, all the times you might have had — but didn't, and now they haunt and taunt you. The deadness you know may be from icy relationships, once warm and filled with hope and possibility, but now as lifeless as the weeds in your flower beds.

Whatever it is that has finished us off and crushed any sense of joy in living out of us, we know those moments, those places. And knowing them, being there, we'd like to be somewhere else and know something else — like, be in a place of surging new life and know new beginnings. We'd like to hear someone say, "The longing and waiting are over; new life is ready to burst forth!"

Right, we may have trouble saying it, but God doesn't! This is God's glorious, life-renewing Good News for us today. God's intention and power to renew knows no limits, and certainly not ours. We may say we're finished, dead, frozen, lifeless, and without hope, but those are not words God knows; God isn't finished with any of us yet!

Whatever else Scripture is saying to us today, surely it is saying this. When Paul says that we are a new creation in Christ, that the old has passed away and the new has come, this is exactly what he means. It is what God has done for us in Christ, and it makes a huge difference in how we live — today, tomorrow, and all the other tomorrows. It means that within us is that constantly renewing, creative power of God's love that is always at work transforming us, transforming the places of cold deadness into places of surging life.

How is this? How is it that we get to this place? Listen again to Paul, and let him teach us, for there is no better teacher. This is because if there was anyone who ever knew both sides of it — deadness and life — it was Paul. He knew what it was like to live in the midst of his own failures and disappointments, all of the bad choices he had made. He knew the struggle of trying to make sense out of what often looks like one senseless day stretching into another one. Paul knew about dead-end living, and he knew his own inability to do anything about it. This is what he means in the text when he talks about "the human point of view," or literally, "looking at things according to the flesh." What he means is "looking at life without being transformed by the renewing power of God in Christ Jesus." That perspective is looking on life and living it left to ourselves and wrapped up in ourselves. *Then* we see only the "same old, same old." We see only our predicament of failure and our impotence to do anything about it. Then we know only one meaningless day after another; we know only the "should haves" and "could haves," all of the dead-end living we've created for ourselves. And we hear only our own cries of despair and desperation, that we're finished, and all we will ever see, know, and hear is what we see, know, and hear now.

Paul knew, however, that God doesn't know those words; God has something else to say to us. And you will notice that the emphasis is on God: God takes the initiative; God reaches to us, even when we cannot reach beyond ourselves; God bridges the gap we cannot, and like the Father in Luke's story of the Prodigal Son (which really is misnamed; the story should be called the story of the Forgiving Father), God — always waiting, always watching for us to come home — runs to embrace and renew, saying the words we so desperately long to hear, "I'm not finished with *any* of you yet!"

As Paul himself discovered, the word is spoken in Christ. Through love divine and grace amazing, we are healed, set free from ourselves and our failures, made new. Oh, sure, we still struggle. Paul knew this; he knew that we are not fully completed by the grace of Christ, that we are living in the midst of the old creation in terms of the new one God has brought about in Christ.

We are still human, and so, in Paul's words, we often fall back into looking at things from a human point of view. But, praise God, *God* looks at us differently, and with love, in and through Christ, renews us for the living. No wonder Paul took his ministry so seriously. If you have heard these words, how can you keep them inside, how can you not want someone else to hear them?

How about us, in this time and place, do we hear them, really hear them, words of hope and new beginnings? Or, do we hear only ourselves, or perhaps everyone else saying, "Give it up! You're finished; there will never be anything any different; you will never be different!"?

Listen! Listen ever so carefully, with expectation and hope reborn within you, for God really is saying something to us this day, saying something that will transform our lives and liberate us from the winter of our discontent.

God is saying, "I'm not finished with you!" It is a distinctly personal word. You see, God doesn't just care for the few, or special, or privileged. God cares for each and every single person! So God's renewing and life-giving power in Christ is for *you*, for each and every *one* of us. God isn't finished with any of us, and God is ready and willing to make each of us into something new; it is a personal word, distinctly for you.

God is saying, "Your past is wiped away." Really. There really are no limits to God's power to renew and transform life. It does not matter what you have done, or where you have been; it doesn't matter how far you've run from God or from yourself. It doesn't matter how much ugliness is in your life, God sets it aside; God's love erases the past and creates a new, fresh future for every single one of us!

God is saying, "You can be new!" Wouldn't you want to be? Wouldn't you like to make a new beginning — not just today, but every day yet to come, to let newness surge through you? God says it is real; it is real for us because there are no limits to the renewing power of grace. Even today does not limit grace, for God promises the power and presence of Christ to be with us each day — this one, as well as all those to follow. God isn't finished and never will be, until all humanity and all creation are held within the embrace of the One who never, never stops loving.

This is news for which we've all been waiting. The moment has come. On this "star date," and every star date of our lives, God has crossed our path. This is the place and time when light banishes the darkness we have known and deadness is transformed into life. In God's power we are brought to this place, and the waiting — for us — is over. Now only God waits and listens for the words we really do know. They are simply, "Yes, Lord; I'm coming home."

If You're Going To Get There, You've Got To Leave Here

Philippians 3:4b-14

Cokie Roberts, Chief Congressional Analyst for ABC News and a national correspondent for National Public Radio, can tell you more than the latest challenge facing the President and the latest on a crisis somewhere in the world. She can also tell you about how, if you're going to move on to where you want to be, you've got to let go of where you are.

She knows this out of both personal and professional experience, and Cokie Roberts has put this knowledge to use in an arena not as publicly known as her work with Sam Donaldson or Bob Edwards. Since 1994, Cokie Roberts has been the Moderator for Hospice Foundation of America's annual national teleconference. As you are aware, Hospice Foundation of America, and their local chapters, is committed to enabling persons and their families to deal with death and dying, the terminally ill, and especially with grief following the death of a loved one. Cokie Roberts has a stake in this and personal knowledge of the pain of grief. She knows the long transition one goes through in the grieving process, for she endured the premature death of her own sister in 1991.

So she has been there. She knows what she's talking about. She knows the journey. Cokie Roberts knows that a large part of living has to do with learning how to say, "Good-bye," so we can bring ourselves to say, "Hello," again.

You and I (at least implicitly) know it, too. We know it not only in processing grief, but we also know it in other dimensions of our life experience. The whole point in rearing children is to say, "Good-bye," to them — to get them to the point where they can strike out on their own as independent adults. If you and I are to grow as persons, we *have* to grow! That is, we need to let go of one level of maturation — and not be stuck there — so we can grow on to another. This is true in our personal relationships with friends or with a life partner. No relationship stays the same; it either grows and develops — moving on — or it stultifies and dies. It is, of course, true in our professional lives: to move on to new challenges, new opportunities and advancement, we have to leave behind where we've been. We cannot say, "Hello," to something new without first saying, "Good-bye," to what was.

Indeed, this is one of those "rock bottom" truths we need to master in living if our lives are going to have any authenticity and growth, and it's one of those critical lessons in living parents need to teach their children: most of the time you have to let go of one thing to be able to grasp a new thing. Before you can say, "Hello," to a new, fresh, life-giving experience, you've got to say, "Good-bye," to what has been in its way. If you're going to get *there*, you've got to leave *here*!

We know this, even though sometimes we forget it, even though sometimes we are intentional about forgetting it. Sometimes we just plain resist the truth of it, stubbornly believing that — one, we don't *have* to let go of what has been to experience what might be, or two, we don't have to go anywhere. That is to say, we've already arrived; we are perfectly complete — and happy, and fulfilled, and everything else — just where we are.

It is an illusion! It is an illusion that will impede our fulfillment as human beings in every dimension of our lives, and it is an illusion that will especially block our fulfillment in our spiritual journey.

Whether or not Cokie Roberts knows this, Paul did — in both his personal and spiritual life — and we can learn something from him, something important and useful for our journey. His own words strip away every mask behind which he might have hidden, and they are the intensely personal words we find in his letter to the Philippians.

There, Paul talks about the transformation which has taken place in his life. He lifts up his heritage — what was — and it's very impressive: born into Judaism (not a convert), of the leading tribe of Benjamin — the tribe that gave Israel her first king; reared in a solid, orthodox family; a member of the sect in Judaism (the Pharisees) whose sole purpose was to achieve a righteous life by keeping all of the Jewish Law — and Paul did! He had achieved this, and in his zeal committed himself to stamping out every heresy, every threat to his faith. This is what was, where Paul had been.

And then it happened. He encountered the Risen Christ, and in that encounter his life changed. Yes, but the transition did not come without letting go of what was. All of that — even his exalted heritage — was in the way. The privilege, status, and power he knew before was a roadblock to where Christ was calling him to be. Paul knew that the new life of joy and hope, of authenticity and meaning that Christ promises cannot come without some letting go; that kind of transition requires some "good-byes." To get *there* always challenges us to leave *here*.

It was all both clear and inescapable for Paul. He knew he had to set some new priorities in his living, letting go of what was, so he could grasp what might be. In his own words he said it this way: "For the sake of my relationship with Christ I have suffered the loss of all things, and count them as refuse, in order that I may gain Christ and be found in him" (Philippians 3:8-9).

You'll also notice — and this is tremendously important — that the "letting go" wasn't just a once-and-for-all act: it was continual; it was (and is) process. Paul knew that he hadn't arrived yet, that there was no place on the journey (because it *is* a journey!) that you could just sit down and complacently say, "Well, I've got *this* down." No. Paul uses the metaphor of a race, a race that doesn't end until our completion in the very presence of God, to describe the journey. Again, let the profound eloquence of his own words penetrate our thinking: "Not that I've already obtained perfection in Christ, but I press on to make it my own, because Christ has made me his own. Friends, I do not consider that I've arrived; but one thing I do: forgetting what lies behind and straining toward that which lies ahead I press toward the goal for the prize of the heavenly call of God in Christ Jesus" (Philippians 3:12-14).

This was Paul's life; this was his experience. Searching for something that would give his life meaning and authenticity, he finally found it. Longing for joy in his life, rather than the nagging emptiness he knew (yes, "emptiness," for regardless of what he had achieved, Paul could not escape from his own feelings that there's got to be something more out there, something more to living) — longing for joy and not emptiness, for hope and not despair, this was Paul's experience.

What about you and me? What about our experience? Are you stuck in a dead-end life, a life empty of joy and meaning? Do you struggle with boredom and weariness with it all, just seeing one more day melt into another? Has despair claimed you, claimed you to the point where your own life is absolutely void of joy and hope?

If this is where you are — and most of us are either there, have been there, or are on our way there — then God has a word for you today. In our own unfulfilled living, our own struggle with meaning, purpose, and direction, God has some good, life-transforming, hope-generating news for us: We can get there! We, too, can experience transition in our lives; we can move from emptiness to joy, from aimlessness and boredom to purpose and meaning, from despair to hope. It can happen! We, too, can have a life-giving, life-transforming relationship with Christ!

Yes, but we can't get *there* without leaving *here*, and the journey will always be a journey. Knowing this, know also how we can put it in place in our own living. There are four essential steps.

The first step is to recognize clearly and acknowledge where you presently are. Mark's story of the healing of Blind Bartimaeus in the tenth chapter of his Gospel is marvelously helpful to us here. When Bartimaeus hears Jesus is near, he cries out to him. He cries out to him because he knows he has a need — he is blind — and he knows Jesus can meet the need. And so when Jesus poses the question, "What do you want me to do for you?" Bartimaeus does not hesitate. He says, "Master, let me receive my sight." And Mark goes on to say, "Immediately he received his sight and followed him on the way" (Mark 10:52). Bartimaeus got it! He knew that the first step to seeing is to acknowledge your blindness. The first step to wholeness is to realize you *aren't*, and the first step to getting *there* is to recognize and acknowledge you are *here*. So it is for you and me: if we are to get *there* — to the place of wholeness and joy and hope and all the rest — we need to first recognize we are *here*. This is primary.

The second step once we realize and acknowledge we are here, we aren't there — is to want to *be* there. This is the step of desire. It is the heartfelt, burning desire within to be somewhere else than where we presently are. And if we don't have the desire, we aren't going to go or be anywhere different from where we are now. To get there, you have to want to get there.

Then — once we've faced where we really are, once we've decided we want to be somewhere else in our living — then we have to act on it. This is the step of intentionality. You see, if we "see," and if we want to go to the new place we see, we've got to be intentional about it. We've got to *do* something, to act on our desire, to let go. It simply will not happen without it. No one else can take us there. We will not get there by wishing it or just hoping it. We move from here to there *by* moving: by the intentional choice to let go so we *can* go.

And the going — this side of being in the presence of God — never ends. The journey *is* a journey. We never get to the place when we can just sit down and complacently rest, thinking we've arrived. No, the fourth step from getting here to there is actually the fifth, sixth, and on and on — because the journey is on and on, on toward completeness in Christ.

Not on ABC, nor on NPR, this is the news God has for us today. If you are stuck in your life — stuck in the boredom and emptiness of your days, stuck in despair and hopelessness — you can get un-stuck. God has something more in mind for you, something rich and good, something filled with hope and joy. But let me — and Cokie Roberts and Paul and everyone else who's been stuck at one time or another — let me tell you: If you're going to get *there* — you're going to have to leave *here*.

The Power That Brings Victory

Philippians 2:5-11

There are no exceptions: Every single person in Jonesboro, Arkansas — and maybe every single person in this nation — would like to grip as tightly as possible the minute hand on the clock, holding it at 12:34 p.m., on March 24, 1998. This is because at 12:35 p.m. a horror of destruction and violence was unleashed that changed lives forever. 12:35 p.m. was the moment when the hand of eleven-year-old Andrew Golden pulled the fire alarm at Westside Elementary School, putting into motion fifteen minutes of terror which left five lives ended forever, blotting out what was good and filled with hope, leaving an aftermath of incredible pain and all kinds of unanswered questions.

It is not my intention today to answer them. None of us have any certainty about why children become killers. Oh, sure, I have a lot of feeling about this and some ideas about the cause; like the availability of weapons in this country, like the constant bombardment of media violence, like the cheapening of human life, and so on. Nonetheless, the complete and absolute truth about this tragic episode will remain elusive for us.

No, my intention is not to speculate about that which remains elusive; it is, rather, to focus heart and mind on that which is *not* speculative, nor elusive, but is the bedrock truth, a truth every single one of us here and everywhere else needs to know and understand. This is the truth: one, the less we know victory in living, the more we search for the power that will bring it. Two, the more we lodge power in violence and control over others, the more destructive our lives become, and the more elusive the victory is. And three,

God has shown us where authentic power really lies, how victory can be ours, and how both the power and the victory can transform not only our lives, but this world in which we live.

The events in Jonesboro, Arkansas, may appear farther removed from us than just by the physical distance, but they are in fact connected to us just as closely as the violence you saw on last night's local news broadcast or read about in this morning's newspaper. It doesn't matter if it's eleven-year-old or thirteen-year-old children shooting twelve-year-old children, or terrorists blowing up buses in Israel, or someone being mugged on any street in any city in this nation. All acts of violence are tied together with one thread, and we need to understand this if we are to survive and our children are to survive. The thread is this: a lack of victory in living will inevitably generate a drive to gain power, so the victory can be achieved. It can be the sense of failure and impotence, a lack of self-esteem that pushes a child to say, "I'll show them!" It can be the trauma of losing one's own country through the decision of a world body one cannot control, coupled with fifty years of fanatical paranoia and oppression, as we witness in Palestine. It can be the hopelessness of poverty that issues in a drive toward power and the oppression of the oppressor. It can be any of these, and more, but it's all the same: we live in a world where few know *any* victory in living.

Wait! That's too broad. We live in a community, in a neighborhood, where few know any victory; we go to school and work where few know victory. Oh, it might not look like it; we look around us where we live, go to school and work, and it looks like lots of people know victory: after all, for the most part they are not in poverty, they are not oppressed, they are not powerless victims. But looks can be deceiving, can't they? Looks reveal only the obvious, only what's on the outside. When we penetrate appearance and even our own desperate denial, the truth is there in all of its stark reality: few of us know victory in living. I mean *real* victory: a sense of self-worth, that we count, that we are loved and esteemed; I mean a life that has some meaning and direction and satisfaction to it; I mean having a reason to live at all, and to celebrate the gift of life with joy.

The fact is, it's not there for huge numbers of us; it may not be there for you. And if it isn't, you and I will strive for it; we will search for the power that will bring victory to us, and we will keep searching until we find it.

Tragically, if we find the power in violence, or in control over and manipulation of others, it will prove to be destructive to our lives, and the victory and authentic power we seek will become all the more elusive. Just ask Mitchell Johnson and Andrew Golden if and when they emerge from the criminal justice system. If their act of violence was to win esteem and love and honor from their classmates, it didn't work out this way. If the destruction of five lives was to give them some sense of power and victory, it ended up destroying them. And so it will with us. Violence has rooted within it the seeds of self destruction. We know this is true; we've seen it again and again. When urban riots swept this nation, whose neighborhoods were left looking like a war zone? When violence, and control over others, and brutality claim a community, who are the victims? You see, we forget this. When we are powerless and know only defeat, we wrongly think that if we seize the power — and do to *them* what they did to *us* — we will find the victory. We will not! The victory will remain elusive, and the destructiveness will destroy us.

This is not only worth knowing socially; it is also worth knowing personally. If you — personally — are longing for victory and power in your life (and most of us are!), you're not going to find it by manipulating others, controlling others, lording it over them, or climbing to the top by using everyone around you as ladders. That kind of living destroys relationships, and it will ultimately destroy you, too. This is because love cannot live in the midst of violence and control. Fear? Yes, it can live. Hatred? Sure! Hatred cannot only live in the midst of violence, it thrives on it! But love? Never! And it is love — given and received — that makes relationships possible, *is* the victory, and releases authentic power. Violence and destruction, manipulation and control don't; they lead only to defeat and ultimately death.

This, in its stark simplicity, is not only what the fifteen minutes of horror beginning at 12:35 p.m. on March 24, 1998, teach us; it is what God has been trying to teach us for almost 2,000 years. It is a lesson about what looked like victory, but wasn't; what looked like defeat, but wasn't; what *real* victory — and the power that really brings it — really was and is. You see, in Christ God has made a statement about what real power is and how it is unleashed. All evidence to the contrary, it is love that overcomes violence and destruction, and brings the victory.

This was the lesson God was teaching through those events of so long ago, which we now call "Holy Week." Those present when Jesus made his entrance into Jerusalem didn't quite get it. They thought *this* was the victory! They thought that God was finally going to straighten things out, throw off the hated oppressors from Rome, and bring back the glory days of what used to be. They were dead wrong. This was not the victory, because the victory isn't won riding on a donkey; it isn't won with shouts of praise ringing in your ears; this is not how power is unleashed.

If we follow the Gospel's chronology literally, those who witnessed a few days later on Good Friday what was good and filled with hope blotted out thought *they* got it. They thought the victory belonged to violence and brutality. They thought that power was being in control over a simple carpenter, and all the power belonged to the mighty and strong. They were dead wrong, too. It was only those touched and claimed by the power unleashed on the Cross and confirmed three days later that *really* got it.

Paul was one of those, and few have expressed the truth God taught on the Cross more powerfully than did Paul in the lesson we read from Philippians. If we are going to get it, we need to hear him with clarity. Paul says that authentic victory comes in emptying yourself *of* self, and living a life of radical obedience to God. Paul says that this is what Jesus did, that he was faithful to God's way of self-giving love to the very end of his life. In doing so, the most amazing thing happened: what looked like defeat was transformed into victory; those who appeared to have power were left impotent; death itself was found as powerless as the violence that brought it; and true power — the power that brings victory — was unleashed forever! This is what Jesus' death on the cross meant: it is self-giving love that is the victory; victory lies nowhere else. This is what God has been trying to teach us all along.

The lesson was not easy to learn; it still isn't. Everywhere surrounding us, as it was for everyone who surrounded the Cross on Golgotha, are all kinds of reasons to believe that power is in violence, and those with the will to power will be the winners. Disgruntled, self-serving religious leaders and their rabble can blot out life — what is good and filled with hope — as easily as can a thirteen-year-old and an eleven-year-old child. There are few exceptions to those who think violence and self-assertion are the power that brings victory.

Yes, but those who shout a resounding "No!" in the face of violence and self-centeredness; those who dare to have, in the words of Paul, "the mind of Christ," emptying themselves, pouring out life and investing love, they know different! They have learned the hard lesson that it is love given away that unleashes the power that brings victory; there *is* no other way! Dear friends, if we are to know victory — in our lives, in this church, in this world where God has placed us an instruments of love, there *is* no other way! For this, and for us, there are no exceptions.

The Hands That Hold Hope

1 Corinthians 11:23-26

"Personal" is the operative word. Everything about the evening, and for that matter, everything before and after it, was intensely personal. Purge from your mind the stylized formal room with the big, long table, and the guests frozen in groupings of threes, with the host framed in the middle. With all of that in the way you will not see what *he* saw. And what Jesus saw, bathed in the flickering, golden light of oil lamps, maybe with a candle or two added, was intensely personal. There was Simon — not "Peter," but the other one, the one who translated everything Jesus said into a political program. Matthew (or "Levi," as some called him) was there, still struggling to get his mind out of the box of his rigid, sterile tradition, and Jesus loved him for it. He looked into the eyes of the inner circle, and saw them — personally — for who and what they were: Peter, coarse and vulgar, but filled with passion and promise; the Zebedee brothers, James and John, egotistical, whose sibling rivalry extended to the others as if they were blood kin, too. He saw the face of Thomas, and he knew that not even his own personal charisma could drive the skepticism away. The others stared back at him, trying to penetrate the moment; and then his eyes locked with Judas, and in that one pregnant moment they both knew how intensely personal it all was.

Do *we* know how personal, how intensely personal, it all is? To wrestle with that question is to probe and be probed with what difference (if any) it will make for us when *we* receive the Bread and Cup. To answer the question is to know what difference (if any) this will make for this world around us.

Whatever else happened in the Upper Room among Jesus and his disciples "on the night when he was betrayed," whatever else went on before the tradition was molded by its various theological nuances, what happened was intensely personal: it was an act *by* a person, *for* persons. What was done was first done for individuals, all twelve of them, even for Judas the betrayer, done for each and everyone individually *by* an individual.

This is so important for us to grasp because it really lies at the core of what our Christian faith proclaims in the dramatic event of the Lord's Supper in the Upper Room. We proclaim something personal. Our faith as Christians is not rooted in abstract, esoteric propositions about an amorphous power totally transcendent to us, but our faith is intensely personal. It is rooted in a historical person. We proclaim a God who enters into the historical process, into the lives of persons. We proclaim a God who did this definitively in a person, who gathered persons around him, creating a community of persons who then reached out to individuals to share — "proclaim" — the story personally. All of this is embedded in the tradition Paul received, then passed on to the Christians at Corinth, and of which Paul reminds them in the text. In Paul's mind the topology of the Lord's Supper is clearly the topology of the Exodus narrative of the Passover, coupled with that of the covenant at Sinai (Exodus 24:8), and joined with the promise of the "New Covenant" in that magnificent passage from Jeremiah: "Behold, the days are coming, says the Lord, when I will make a new covenant with the house of Israel and the house of Judah ... I will write it upon their hearts ... for they shall all know me ... for I will forgive their iniquity, and I will remember their sin no more" (Jeremiah 31: 31-34). Paul, and apparently the tradition before him, recognized that in the death of Jesus in the shedding of *his* blood and not that of animals, God had effected a new act of liberation, for *all* humanity and not for just one ethnic group. Moreover, in this act of divine deliverance all human estrangement from God has been overcome, and a new relationship with God — a New Covenant — has been established.

The power of it all, however, is released when we begin to see that the whole life-liberating, community-creating, hope-giving experience is rooted *in a person*. Let its power touch us: the Exodus centered on a divine *act*; the promised New Covenant was focused on what *God* would do; yes — but the tradition Paul lifts up is centered *in a person*. To be sure, it is centered in a person who is an instrument of God's purposes, but it nevertheless is intensely personal. Jesus says, "This is *my* body given for *you*; this is the New Covenant *I* have made possible in the pouring out of *my* life; it is for *you*." And, as Paul says, it is not some ritualistic act, but it is the *Lord's* death we proclaim! "Personal" is the operative word.

It is the operative word for you and for me. Yes, it's the operative word for the whole of humanity, but today (and every day of our lives) the whole of humanity begins *with us*. Let your mind and heart pull it all forward into this present moment. More than a Loaf, more than a Cup, those hands held hope; and they hold hope for each and everyone of us personally in *this* place, in *this* moment.

It is hope for liberation, for deliverance for us in our bondage. No chains link us to a tyrant ruler; our bondage is more subtle than that. We are held captive by empty and meaningless lives. Oh, not that we haven't tried to pump them with value! We fill our days with frenetic activity; we fill our bank accounts and stock portfolios; we fill our homes and garages with so much stuff we have to go out and rent other places to store it ... and we are *still* empty! It is bondage! Investing our lives and our love in self, we find no return; held captive by a culture that worships image, we are left clueless as to who we really are. Christ sets us free from such emptiness; Christ delivers us from the boredom of our empty lives! The hopeful word of liberation, spoken in the Upper Room, is ours to hear in this place, in this moment: the issue is not what you have; the issue is *whose you are!* And we are persons — individuals — Christ gave himself to liberate from dead lives, finding meaning and purpose that we are of ultimate worth in the eyes of God.

It is liberation and deliverance from our estrangement from God and each other, deliverance from all the hurt we have caused, the unloving lives we have lived. What Christ holds is hope, even for us personally. We are unburdened by the miserable failures of our lives, pointed in a new direction, set on the very threshold of new beginnings. Unchained from our past, delivered from the bondage of lives lived only to self, Christ holds before us the hope of something else: a life finding meaning through love being shared; a life constantly renewed through the unlimited grace of God; a life filled with joy that we count, we count ultimately in the eyes of God; a life lived in community — with God and with other persons. It is a life of hope! All of this is what his hands hold.

Yes, and it is what is held in *our* hands, personally: hope, for each other; hope, for this desperate world where God has called us into community. We hold in our hands hope for each other. It is because we are not only individuals liberated by God and claimed personally for God; we are also individuals *in community* — with God and with each other. Entering into the covenant makes it so, whether it was the one formed at the foot of Sinai, the one that filled Jeremiah's hope, the one made in the Upper Room, the one reenacted at Corinth, or the one in which we participate today. When you and I receive what is delivered to us, we enter into community with each other, as well as with God. And so, what has been delivered to us *can be* delivered to each other. It is hope! We hold it in *our* hands, and when *we* love and forgive, lives are liberated; when we point in the direction *out* of self and into the lives of others, we point those we touch toward lives of meaning and purpose; when we include *all* within the embrace of our arms, we birth hope in those burdened by their sense of unworthiness; hope comes alive!

Why, then, should we think it would be any different for all those not in this place, not next to us in these moments? Hope is not only *our* need; *every* person needs hope for the weary heart, and in our hands we hold such hope. We hold it personally, and in every act of compassion and mercy, in our every act of justice and kindness, we deliver what we have received.

Such is the power that is released when hands are stretched out. Without touching, nothing happens; without delivering, nothing is received. But when one touches another, life is transformed, personally. One link forms another; Jesus' hand grasps Peter's, who reaches to James and John, who touch another and another, until someone's hand grasps Paul's, and he reached out — personally! — to someone in Corinth, and on and on to here, today.

Now, it is in our hands, and "personal" *is* the operative word. Personally, it makes a huge difference in what we do with what we now hold. Purge from your mind the illusion there might be any other way. There never was; there isn't now. It simply takes a Person to deliver what they have received, and when it happens remembering becomes doing, loss becomes gain, death becomes life, and hope is placed in someone's hand and heart.

Good Friday

Peeking Over The Fence

Hebrews 10:16-25

It wasn't quite a race, although there was a noisy, clamoring crowd, a definite course, and an ending, a finish line. The crowd didn't cheer, but jeered. The course wasn't straight at all, nor smooth; there was no hope of getting the wind to his back. It went up and down, twisted and turned, bumped over uneven stones; it was impossibly narrow and difficult at times. And the end, the finish line was a place he'd just as soon not have come to — because it was the end of everything: three years of profoundly difficult work, low moments of despair, as well as exhilarating moments of triumph — just like — what was it? — last Sunday. That was over, and this soon would be. Every hope, every dream, every bond of love and community were now shattered in a shambles of betrayal, flight, and fear. Jesus peered up the hill, and through sweat and blood and tears (his own!) stinging his eyes, he finally saw it: the end; the dead end of this whole up-and-down incredible journey. At least it looked like the end.

Not then, but now; not there, but here, we see it, too: the dead end of our own journey. Even if we haven't gotten there, we can see it. It's out there, and it may be closer than we've ever thought or ever wanted. It looms before us: every hope, every dream, every bond of love shattered and lying in a shambles. You don't have to be Jesus to see it, and it doesn't have to be that first Good Friday, or even this Good Friday, for the dead end to slap you in the face. You can be yourself and see it; you can see it any day, including this one. It is the dead end of your life, with the weight and burden of your own failure on your back — all of the ugly, unloving things you've done, been, and become. The hurtful words you've hurled, the phoniness you've lived, the self-centeredness that has made room only for you, the concern you've had only for you — all of it! — now stands before you. It is the pain and shambles of lost community, broken relationships, and betrayal; it is the dead end that comes when trust leaves. It is the place where and when there is no place left to go.

You and I know it all too well. We've been there often; we'll get there again; some of us are there now. And seeing it all, whether it's near or far, God help us, don't we wish we could see something else? — not a dead end, but a living beginning, something else to see, something like new hopes, new dreams, new life, a new us.

Look, with eyes of faith, and you *can* see it! Peek over the fence, and it stretches before each of us! Jesus did, and saw it, and got there; and God's word of hope and promise to each of us this good day, this Good Friday, is that because he did, we can as well. We can see it and get there if we dare peek over the fence.

With vision blurred just enough to be able to see with the clarity of faith, Jesus' eyes fixed upon it. The cross was no longer on his back, but it was up there before him. Rather than being the ignominious instrument of his degradation, it was the means of his enthronement. It was not the way in which life would leave him and death would come, but just the opposite! It was the means by which *death* would leave him and *life* would come! Yes, and life would come not just to him, but in and through the Cross life would come for us, for all humanity, for all times!

This was the "new thing" the author of Hebrews had in mind when he quoted those stirring words of Jeremiah. This was the new covenant, the new beginning, the "new and living way" that Christ opened to all, and it was there to see in all of its power, there beyond the curtain of our hopelessness and alienation, beyond all the dead ends of our lives. It is God's gift to us; it is what God has done for us, this good day and every day of our lives. When our life reaches a dead end, God shows us another path, a way beyond what we can presently see. Christ opens our eyes to it; Christ beckons us toward it.

Over the fence that blocks our path, beyond the dead end of our days, Christ opens our eyes to it; Christ beckons us toward it. It is the place and time when life will surge through us again, and we shall dream new dreams and know love never betrayed. It is you and I in the very presence of God. As the writer of Hebrews rightly understood, the place and time of the presence of God is not found in any sanctuary of any ancient temple; neither is it only experienced in some distant heavenly realm, but God's presence is encountered in our present. Here and now we can go beyond where we are and have been, go into God's presence, a presence that can change everything, even us.

In the presence of God we find welcome, and not rejection. With arms wide enough to embrace us and all the world, God welcomes us as God's own child. Set aside are all the words that have told us we are unwanted, not good enough, not "something" enough, and in their place are the words that welcome us to the place of love and healing.

It is because in the presence of God we encounter the One who accepts us without condition. It is the scandal of the Gospel! We do not have to prove ourselves to be worthy of society with God; God proclaims that no one, not us nor anyone else, is unfit for society with God. We do not have to first fix ourselves up, hoping that then God will embrace us; God fixes us! Nothing we have ever done or will do bars us from the presence of God; nothing we have been or might become excludes us. God's loving presence invites, accepts, welcomes all; none are left out, none are fenced off. "Just as I am" is more that a wistful, plaintive plea; it is the way God welcomes all into God's renewing presence.

And it *is* a renewing presence! With God we discover the healing of our fractured lives; dead ends are behind us; new beginnings are before us. Now if you have no need to be "sprinkled clean" or "washed pure" (to use the words of the Epistle), this will mean nothing to you. If there is no longing within you for the days to come when there is no remembrance, by you *or* God, of your sins and misdeeds (as Jeremiah described his own people's dead end), this holds no power for you. But if you are where most of us are — burdened by the "should haves" and "could haves" of our days, embarrassed by our own failures, broken and bleeding inside from the mess we've made of things, seeing nothing but the wreckage of our lives — why, then, this is glorious Good News! God sees more than this! God sees a person of ultimate value and worth, who in the powerful presence and love of God can know healing, wholeness, and renewal. When you and I are in that presence we see it, too: not a dead end, but a life beginning!

We see a life beginning to discover meaning and purpose and joy. This is what is found in the presence of God. It is what happens when we discover a love for us without bounds, realizing that in the eyes of God none are without worth, all are accepted simply for who and what they are: God's precious children. When we discover this depth of love we discover the healing of our hurts; the past is set aside, and we can embrace a new future. It is the experience of joy that comes with knowing we count, we count ultimately to God; and because we count, our life has purpose; it is the purpose of joyfully living out as instruments of love and healing the grace we have received.

Peering over the fence, beyond all that has blocked the joy in living we can know, this is what we can see. Far from a dead end — and a dead ending — to be in the presence of God opens a new door of new possibilities for us just when all else would be slammed in our face. No wonder the day it was flung open for you and me and all humanity we call "Good Friday"! What else could it be but "good"?

Such is the confession of our hope, this day and everyday, and it is worth holding onto without wavering. The Epistle is quite right: the One who has promised it *is* faithful, even to us. You see, since Christ has moved beyond all dead ends, even death itself, so can we! Hear God's hope-filled Good News for us: God has healed our alienation; we are a forgiven people; and hence, you and I and everyone who dares to peek over the fence and see what life in the presence of God can be like can in fact enter into it. God has promised it, and God can be trusted to keep the promise.

Sometime or another you will need to know this. When it isn't a race, but a journey you're just trying to survive; when no cheering, but only jeers ring in your ears; when your path is so crooked and rough and uneven you're stumbling all the way; when the burden of your life is too heavy for your heart to bear — and through your own sweat and blood and tears you see nothing but a dead end — *look again! Peek over it*! God is there for you; nothing else matters.

Easter Day

If You Haven't Faced Today, Tomorrow Won't Matter

1 Corinthians 15:19-26

The French are not speaking to each other, and we should be concerned. Vanishing are those French cafés of the 1950s which dotted the streets on the Left Bank of the Seine in Paris, the places where Albert Camus and Jean-Paul Sartre held court, and the exchange of ideas flowed as freely as the wine. Then the French talked to each other, and the air was filled with passion and reparte like the swirling smoke of Gauloise cigarettes. Now there is increasing silence.

Of course, the French never talked to us, and if you've traveled in France, particularly in Paris, and you cannot speak the language, you know this; they will stare down their patrician noses at you like you're from another planet! But not speaking to each other? *This* is serious! A recent study revealed that ten years ago the French engaged in conversation fifteen percent more frequently than now. Coupled with the disappearance of the café (some 5,000 disappeared from Parisian streets last year alone), this *is* serious. It is serious because France already has the highest rate of suicide of any European country, and being socially isolated from other people simply exacerbates their own sense of hopelessness and alienation.

This is why the French not speaking to each other is serious and why it is seriously important for us, here in this place, on this Easter Sunday. It did not take Camus, Sartre, and the other Existentialists to discover that meaning and hope are essential to human existence, not to conclude that suicide is the only real philosophical question — that is, "Why live at all?" We already knew this. Ever since human beings got to the point of being able to eat without being eaten, and we could enjoy the luxury of reflecting on living rather than just trying to survive, we have known that meaning, purpose, and hope are as essential to living as is the air we are now breathing, or the ham we are going to be eating later. We know it now. There is no reason to live without meaning, purpose, and hope; it's just too painful, too difficult, too ambiguous. Without meaning, purpose, and hope we might as well let the ultimate silence claim us.

Yes, the French are not speaking to each other, but we ought to be! We ought to be saying there is a reason to break the silence, and saying that there is more than the ultimate silence. We ought to be saying that love is worth the risk and relationships are worthwhile. We ought to be speaking to each other and to everyone around us, boldly and courageously saying that life is worth living, even though we sometimes struggle saying that. We ought to be saying that life can be filled with meaning, purpose, and hope, even though sometimes we wonder about that; we ought to be saying this day can be filled with joy, regardless of the sadness that may be in your heart this morning.

We ought to be speaking to each other and to everyone around us today, because if we haven't faced today, tomorrow won't matter. *Today* is the day we need to hear all of this — all of this about meaning and purpose, hope and joy — because today is where we are, and today is tough — for each and everyone of us. I do not know what your hurts are this morning, but I know you have them, even as I have mine. It may be the hurt of loneliness and isolation; it might be the pain of a broken or lost relationship. The hurt might come from some ugly, unloving thing you've done — or was done to you — but whatever it is, it is there with the power to silence joy and kill hope. I do not know the inner struggle with meaning and purpose you are experiencing, but I know it's there inside, even as it is inside me. In the face of suffering and tragedy, illness and the death of those we love; in the midst of all the inexplicable things that happen to us and all the unanswered questions that cry out for answers, we do wonder if life really makes any sense; sometimes it doesn't! I do not know where hope and joy are the hardest for you, but when we are both honest with ourselves, honest with each other — and, yes, honest with God — we both know the truth of it: in the face of hurt, failure, and death itself hope is not easy; when our lives are battered, broken, and stretched, joy seems the rarest of all commodities.

This is where we are today, and it is today when we need more than pious platitudes and certainly more than silence. Today we need to hear and know about meaning and purpose, hope and joy. This cannot wait for tomorrow, for if we cannot find handles on today, tomorrow isn't going to matter to any of us.

You and I are in the right place, at the right time, not only to speak to each other, but also to let God speak to us. And God has been speaking, speaking the words of meaning and purpose, hope and joy; God has been speaking ever since that first Easter morning. God has been and is saying that love is worth the risk and relationships are worthwhile, that life is worth living, that life can be joyous, meaningful, and hope-filled, even and especially in the face of life's most difficult moments, even and especially in the face of death itself. This is the word God has definitively spoken in the life, death, and resurrection of Jesus, a word that powerfully proclaims this day that the Easter faith is not so much for tomorrow as it is for today.

Today, the voice of God meets us in the words of Paul, as we read them together in his letter to the Corinthians. Paul wrote to a people in a crisis of hope. Jesus had not come back in the way they had expected; neither had God's Kingdom come. It just appeared to be the "same old, same old." They were still hurting; they still knew failure and brokenness; and to make matters worse, friends and relatives were still dying around them. Their faith, already fragile — as is ours! — was wavering, in serious jeopardy: After all, if Jesus hadn't come back, maybe he wasn't going to; maybe everything else we believed was wrong; maybe this whole business of resurrection and a living Christ was also wrong; maybe you just struggle in living, and you die, and none of it makes any sense or means anything. Maybe.

Facing it all, Paul had some important things to say; I want to lift up four of them. First, Paul says that Christ's victory over death is a fact, a fact through which God has vindicated the power of love. You'll notice that Paul doesn't describe or debate the "how" of resurrection; none of the Christian writers do. Paul doesn't even know the story of the empty tomb; Luke and the others who have this tradition are much later than Paul. But this isn't important to Paul: not the empty tomb, nor the "how." What is important is the fact of a living Christ whose presence we experience in the Spirit. This isn't a debatable issue for Paul; it is rather a real, living experience of the Living and Risen Christ in our own lives. And through the resurrection of Jesus, Paul says God has made a statement about where victory lies: it lives in love — and love is victorious over all, even over death itself; this is first.

Secondly, Paul says that even though right now the victory of love isn't quite complete, it has been won, and it will come in its completeness. In Paul's mind this is why we — not Christ, but we — still struggle, hurt, fail, and even die. Christ's victory hasn't completely transformed all existence yet, but it will! You can count on it.

Thirdly, and this is tremendously important, Paul says that because of Christ's victory — the victory of love — we, in Christ, shall share in it — not only ultimately, in its completeness, but we can and shall share in it now! Those who are a part of Christ will live, and already are living, the resurrected life! Just as Christ found victory in the power of love, we shall know victory in the power of love; this, too, is a fact.

Lastly, Paul proclaims that if we shall share in the victory, and even are sharing in it now, we can live now with confidence, joy, and hope. We, in this present moment, know now the life-giving power of love. We know now that our lives are going somewhere, that there is purpose and meaning in living, that life can make some sense after all. And because we know all of this now — that God's love in Christ is ultimately victorious, and we shall be, too — we can face the "now" — today — with hope.

Hear with hope what Paul is saying: death — in all of its forms: not just the cessation of breath, but dead dreams, dead useless lives, a heart stilled from hurt, the places of our lives where truly life has vanished and we are in the tombs — death in all its forms and all of its power has no power over us. It has no power today! This is

Paul's answer to the Messengers at the tomb: "Why seek the living among the dead?" (Luke 24:5). You don't! You seek, and find, the Living One in *your* living, for this is where life is found and death is defeated — today! And if you don't seek and find it today, tomorrow isn't going to matter.

Can we really trust in this? Or, like those who heard the news on the first Easter simply think that it's an idle tale, what the text in Luke 24:11 calls literally "the ravings of someone in delirium"? I don't know the answer to that for you, any more than you know the answer for me. We cannot answer this question for each other, but only for ourselves, personally. I do know this, however: if we don't have an answer today, tomorrow isn't going to matter. You see, Paul was right about something else: hope — without fulfillment today — is worse than no hope at all. It is because today is the day we have; this one; and we have to deal with it before we can face any others.

Look, then, at the calendar with care. It says *today* — not yesterday, not tomorrow — but *today* is Easter. In the silence that surrounds us God has spoken, shouted to the world, "Christ is risen; Christ is risen, indeed!" Lift your voices, Easter people! Today we really do have something to say to each other, to say to this desperate world gripped in its own silence. For if it is the Christians who are not speaking to each other today, no tomorrow will matter to anyone!

When The Wailing Ends

Revelation 1:4-8

No cavalry rode to the rescue; this time the savior was technology. Here is how it happened. Longing for more intimate communication between preacher and congregation, the church purchased and installed a wireless microphone system. With an FM receiver in place and wearing a lapel microphone, the preacher could get out from behind the pulpit or lecturn and roam about, even into the midst of the congregation. All worked well until one Sunday morning, while offering the Pastoral Prayer at the altar, over the pastor's voice came a distinct wailing: the whimpering cries of an infant, eerie and disembodied. Suddenly it vanished, only to return later during the sermon. For three weeks in succession this happened, with the congregation becoming more spooked than annoyed. Then it became known what the origin was of these mysterious sounds of anguish. Near the church was the house of a family with a small infant. To monitor the baby while it was in the crib, Mom and Dad had installed — you guessed it — an electronic device that operated on the same FM frequency as did the church's wireless microphone system. The wailing, however, wasn't nearly as interesting as the conversations of truckers *also* picked up by the system. Words were then heard in church unlike any in Holy Scripture! All, however, was laid to rest — the whimpering, the wailing, and the cursing — by the simple flick of a switch and a higher tech sound system.

Don't you wish it was that easy for us? You and I both know it doesn't work that way. It doesn't work that way because of what starts the wailing in the first place. And it isn't a baby in a crib. No, its closer to home than all of this; it is intensely personal; it is us, in the midst of our own living. Our cries of despair and anguish are born from the emptiness of our weary days. The wailing rises from our inability to discover any real sense of meaning and direction in our own living. We wrestle with it, searching for something that will bring us purpose; something that will bring us joy; something that will liberate us from our own isolation, help us to connect and feel we count as persons.

Then, if we really do begin to get ourselves together, to penetrate what really does count in living, when we finally do see the path clearly, we wail because of the wrong turns we make. Sometimes they are turns away from others, away from reaching to someone else, loving someone else — and we turn into ourselves and care only for ourselves. Sometimes the turns are toward destructiveness — of ourselves and those around us. These are turns of addiction, of abuse, of acting out. It's not that we don't *know* better; we *do*! We just don't *do* better!

And the wailing, the cursing starts. Our cries well up from failure, and the hurt we've caused — as well as known from others. Disappointments, unfulfilled dreams, dashed hopes — all of it — starts the wailing, and we long for it to end. We long for new opportunities, for the healing of our broken hearts and battered spirits. We long for new directions in living. We long to make sense out of what sometimes looks so senseless. We long for hope and courage. In the struggle of our days, we long for some reason to stop wailing and start living.

Rising above our cries of anguish God speaks the word of hope and courage. Hear it with joy: whatever cries of disappointment and anguish well up within us over misdirected and empty living, over choices made and consequences suffered, Christ ends the wailing! Bringing grace and peace, the way of hope and renewal, Christ is always coming to those who dare to look for him.

This is what makes the difference. It has always made the difference for the Christian community, but seldom has it made more of a difference than it did to those to whom John the Seer first wrote. This strange piece of writing we call "the Revelation to John" comes to us from the time of the close of the first century. As does all apocalyptic literature, it had its birth in the crucible of extreme persecution, real doubt about the future, and deep anxiety over the present. John's church was at the mercy of a madman. Domition, Emperor of Rome, claimed divinity for himself and the brutal oppression and execution of all who did not bow to his sway. Caught squarely in the middle were the Christians. Their calling was to worship God alone; their way was the Way of Jesus, the Way of the Cross, not the way of violence. And caught in the middle, it was a profound crisis for their faith. "Where is God in the midst of all of this?" they questioned. "If God is in charge — or even cares — why is this happening to us?" they wondered. "Is faith — faith in God, faith in Christ — is it possible in a world like ours?" they wailed.

Hearing their wailing and cursing, John wrote words of faith and hope: "Grace to you and peace...." Really? "Grace and peace" in the face of all we are facing? "Grace and peace" in the midst of our shattered lives? How can this be? Where is there any grace, any peace?

It can be and is found because John knew the truth of it all; it had been revealed to him! John knew that *God* was in charge, and that God was and is a God of history, always coming to enter the history of God's people with renewing love. Yes, God's purposes can be opposed. God's purposes can be slowed down and sidetracked; but they cannot be defeated, because the victory of love has already been won! When Jesus died on the Cross in absolute faithfulness to the Way of love, and when God raised him to life through the power of God's love, the victory was won!

This is God's statement about life! Love triumphs, not hatred and violence. Life triumphs, not death. This is the gift of grace and peace John sent to his beleaguered church, from "Jesus, the faithful witness (read "martyr" and "victor"), the *first*born of the dead," whose victory they also would inherit upon his coming. Hearing this made a huge difference to John's people in the midst of their weariness, in the crisis of their faith, when all hope was challenged, and all that could be heard was the wailing of God's struggling people.

It makes a huge difference for us. To be sure, no mad emperor threatens our life; no arena of death, filled with wild beasts, waits for us. The crisis is more subtle than this; the wild beasts, though every bit as real, are less obvious. We wonder if God is real and really in charge. We struggle to know if living has any meaningful direction; we wrestle with the meaning of our own suffering. Not those in Asia or Rome, but here, we long to be those who know the victory and receive the gifts of grace and peace from the One who shall bring them when he comes.

Listen, then, and hear the promise again: Christ not only came; Christ not only will come, but Christ is *always* coming with hope and renewal; Christ is *always* coming to those who have the faith to receive him. This is what ends the wailing, whether it started because of our confusion about where the truth of living is really found, or whether the wailing wells up within us because we weren't confused, just plain wrong, and we, like those in John's time, have been the ones who pierced him — whatever started the wailing, Christ's coming to us ends it!

The challenge, of course, is to live in that kind of expectancy, to see and welcome his coming. If Christ really is coming, always coming with hope and renewal to those who dare to look for him — and looking, see both him and the truth he brings — where, then, do we need to look?

John says, "In the clouds." I think it's closer at hand, as close as your own life, your own lived experience. Look, then, with me; look — not up — but within. Look and see when the wailing, loud as it may have been, ended for you. I can tell you when. It was when someone embraced you, taking your pain upon them. It was when a word of encouragement gave you new hope. It was when forgiveness healed the hurt you caused. The wailing, your wailing, ended when your sense of isolation and alienation were overcome, and someone accepted you just as you are, just for who you are. In a word, your wailing ended when you felt loved. That was Christ coming to you, for this is how, when, and where Christ comes in the gentle touch and warm embrace of love given to you — not deserved, but simply given. As Scripture says, it is how the renewing, life-giving power of the Almighty has come, does come, and will come: in a person. So when love has come to you, know the truth of it: it was, and is, and will be Christ coming to you.

How can we be so sure? Because Jesus said it himself. Hear his words as the Fourth Gospel records them: "I will not leave you desolate; I will come to you. The one who knows and keeps my commandments, I will love that one, and my Father will love that one, and we will come to that one" (John 14:18ff). What is the commandment that makes the coming possible? Why, it is the only commandment Jesus ever gave! It is to love one another.

This is not something way up in the clouds; it is right here, down to earth, where you and I live. Neither is it something pushed off into a remote and distant future. It is here and now: When we love, Christ comes! When we venture out of ourselves and into the lives of others; when we love enough to confront this culture around us with the truth of Christ, the truth about living; when we work for justice and an inclusive society, building bridges that unite and overcome alienation; when you and I pour out our lives, even as did Christ; when we love, Christ comes, Christ really comes, and every eye shall see him.

If his coming is obscured, if still we cannot see him, it is not the clouds we need to see beyond — it is ourselves; it is not our eyes we need to open — it is our heart.

Easter 3

The Power That Cannot Fail

Revelation 5:11-14

You know the phrase. It was created by a famous computer software company, but you and I — and indeed, this nation — resonate with it, not because it's about software, but because it's about hard living: "Where do you want to go today?" Not, "Where do I want my business to go?" or "Where do I want to go in the magical world of cyberspace, with all of its instantaneous knowledge?" No. It's, "Where do I want to go with my life — because it isn't going anywhere, we don't seem to be going anywhere good." It's, "What can I know — really know — about living in this world, my world, the real (not "virtual") world, that's going to take me some place other than where I am, where we are now."

And we know where we are now: families fractured; marriages broken; relationships filled with bitterness, resentment, and anger; lives going nowhere good. We know where we are, and where we are — today — isn't a very happy place. Where do you want to go today? Where do we want to go — today?

Some are saying, "Backwards." These are strong voices, voices that are saying, "We need to get back to the way life, family, school used to be." Back. Not just a few years back, but back at least forty years, back to the Eisenhower years, back to when there wasn't enough diversity to celebrate, much less fear. This was before the unraveling of the 1960s. This was Ozzie and Harriet and the boys solving every family squabble in thirty minutes, and the Cleavers being the perfect family, with June in her pearls, Ward in his suit, Wally and the Beaver in their chairs around the dinner table at 5 p.m. Perfect. Then, the only bad thing that happened at school was someone caught smoking in the restroom; then, Father really did know best.

The rest of us — who didn't have a father at home, or whose mothers didn't have pearls — knew something else. The rest knew that it wasn't really real, anymore than was Buffalo Bob and the Peanut Gallery. But, oh, how we wanted it to be! We still do. We want a perfect family, with perfect moms and dads, perfect children, who are perfect successes in perfect schools. We do not want life cheapened by the exploitation of sex and violence in the media. We do not want lives wasted by drugs and families wasted by divorce and abuse — which is what we've got. Now, not then. All of this is why the voices that would pull us backwards are so powerful.

The problem, of course, is that we can't really go there. Even if it was real — and it wasn't — we still could not go there. That time is done, finished, never to return, anymore than the innocence of our children who now arrive at school greeted by police cruisers, surveyed by video cameras, and return home to empty houses — or worse: to homes filled with anger, bitterness, and the neglect and abuse of parents who don't parent.

Where do you want to go today? Where do you want your family, your children, yourself to go? If we can't go back there, and — God help us! — we don't want to stay here — where?

I think we know where. It is the place where families are whole and where love is really alive. It is where moms are deserving of honor, dads are involved with their children, and children really respect their parents — not out of guilt or fear, but because their parents deserve their respect. It is the place and time where all members of the family are valued for who they are, homes are places of joy, and marriages are life-giving and freeing not life-destroying and controlling. *This* is where we want to go! We can see it; we just desperately long to hear how we can do it, how we can get there.

Listen! There is a voice, a voice calling us, not backwards, where we've been, but both beyond where we are now, as well as calling us to where we want to be, where we can be. It is the voice of one who not only has seen it, but who also can tell us how to get there. His name is John of Patmos, and what he saw, what he has to say to us, can make a difference in our lives today.

John saw beyond where he was. He saw beyond fractured families, beyond children without hope, beyond moms and dads stretched to the limit, beyond a world seemingly gone mad, a world that worshiped at the altar of brutality and violence that cheapens all of human life. John saw a different power. It was (and is) a power greater than hatred and intolerance, a power greater than bombs and guns, a power greater than even death itself. He saw what is really worthy of worship — and it is not violence or hurt. This is what John saw: the power that cannot fail to create human life as God has meant it to be. John saw the power of self-giving love, powerfully visible in the Lamb that was slain, John's symbol for Jesus, whose love was so great that his life was poured out for all the world.

Briefly, enter the vision with him. By his side, you and I are glimpsing a fantastic new world. It is a scene of triumph and victory, of praise and worship. What has triumphed is God's way of self-giving love; what is praised is the victory of life that invests itself, pours out itself that life can come, and all of the created order joins in the chorus: "Worthy is the Lamb who was slain!" Worthy is the Lamb — worthy of honor and blessing and power precisely because he *is* slain! That is to say, in the pouring out of life and love, life with all power and richness and joy comes. This is what John's vision is about: the absolute victory of love and nothing but love.

John saw the truth of it, that only the power of love creates meaningful life, vibrant families, relationships that grow in joy. Such power is not exercised in arrogant control, or self-serving manipulation, but it is released only in self-giving love. It is the truth; it is the true power that cannot fail.

It is the truth for us, the truth that can take us in our lives and in our families where we want to go. It is the power that cannot fail to get us there. This is what Jesus has taught us about creating meaningful life, about creating family in the truest sense of the word. When we look to him, we can see it for us.

We can see what creates a healthy family, even a family of one. Looking to Jesus, we can see it: you're going to have to get outside of yourself! You're going to have to leave your own self-centeredness behind — your concern for *your* happiness, *your* agenda, your *self* — leave it behind, and begin to invest yourself in the other people in your family. And if you are a one person family, this means reaching out of yourself and investing in another person. You cannot have a healthy family without this. If you're so wrapped up in yourself, if you love only yourself and have time and energy and interest only for yourself — "family" will be a nonconcept for you. It takes rising out of yourself, risking yourself in love and vulnerability, and investing yourself in the other members of your family really to *be* a family. Jesus shows us this.

When we look to him, we also can see what creates well-functioning, joy-filled marriages. It is self-sacrifice. Whatever else we see when we look to Jesus, we see this: he gave up himself, even his own life. This is what will make your marriage work. It is being focused on meeting the needs of your spouse, even to the point of sacrificing your own needs. It's living in a relationship of authenticity and openness, not one of games-playing and manipulation or control, where the payoff is getting your own needs met to the sacrifice of your spouse's. Just the opposite! When your marriage is based on mutual self-giving, self-sacrificing love, then and only then will you know the true joy that marriage can bring.

Yes, and we can see something else about family when we look to Jesus. We can see what parenting is supposed to look like. What we see is love in action. I intentionally choose the words: love in action. Not in "feeling," or "sentiment," but action. Jesus' life of love was a life of doing. He didn't just talk about loving, or feel like loving, he did it. His life reflected it. Look at what that can mean in parenting. It means making some hard choices. It means really loving your children, even when it's difficult and love will demand tough guidance. It means being involved in your children's lives and taking responsibility for where they go, and what they do, and with whom they're "going" and "doing." It means loving enough to stop enabling irresponsible behavior; love isn't always "Yes." Sometimes it's "No." It means limits and boundaries and rules, and clear expectations. It means loving them! Loving them more than yourself, or your own easy path of least resistance so they'll like you and think you're cool. It means love in action.

It all works the other way, too. Looking to Jesus also enables us as children to see what honoring a mother or a father is all about. It is an ongoing life of love and honor for your parents. It is not just a one-day affair, where out of guilt or sentiment you buy a card and send some flowers. Three hundred and sixty-five days a year Jesus honored his mother and father. He honored them with a love that recognized their sacrifice. It was a love that accepted them for who they were — even when they were wrong. It was a love that transcended their own failure as parents, and forgave them, knowing all the while that, sure, sometimes parents fail — but it isn't because they don't want to be loving and caring parents, it's just that sometimes our selfishness and bad judgment as parents get in the way, and then what a mom or dad needs is a son or daughter to say, "It's okay; I love you anyway." Love. That's the key word. That's what we see when we look to Jesus.

What we see when we look to Jesus and to what he taught us about authentic power and authentic living is a little bit of heaven on earth — which is the compelling force of John's vision. What John saw was heaven that could be and would be on earth, all in God's own time.

It isn't here now, any more than it has been, even forty years ago. *Then* we'd die from conformity and boredom; now we and our children die from hatred, and guns, and drugs, and all the rest that is taking this country to hell and not heaven.

Yes, but this isn't all that can be or will be. We know the truth of it! What can and will be is the absolute triumph of self-giving love. It is where we can go, even today, because it is the power that cannot fail. Neither can we when we make it our own.

When The Song Can Finally Be Sung

Revelation 7:9-17

Now you can't even trust the police. When I was a child growing up in Texas, everyone knew how to spot the police cars: they were big old Ford Crown Victorias, painted black with white doors, sporting black wall tires with little moon hubcaps — or, if they really wanted to be sneaky and fool you, they were big old Ford Crown Victorias painted gray, with whip antennas and license plates that read "City" on them. You could bet the farm on it. Now all that has changed. Police cars are all different makes and models and colors. Even the State Highway Patrol can now be seen driving sport utility vehicles. Not to be outdone, the Youngstown Police Chief has announced a new weapon in the war on crime. A sleek, sporty, white Chevrolet Camero, outfitted for police use, now awaits the officer who over a period of two weeks can write the most tickets for people playing their car stereo or their boom-boxes too loudly. I feel safer already! All of this is just one more tidal wave in the sea of change that surrounds us.

Thank God, there are some things that are verities, like Big Macs that will clog your arteries, and New York models wearing weird clothes, and people demonstrating exercise machines who obviously don't need them, and most especially what happens in every major league ball park in this country between the top and bottom half of the seventh inning. You know what it is: the stadium organ begins to play those familiar notes, everyone stands up, and swaying to the music all join in singing that familiar chorus, "Take me out to the ball game ..." It doesn't matter what's happening on the field; it doesn't matter whether the home team is ten runs ahead or ten runs behind. When the seventh inning comes, it's time to sing! The music plays; the words come on the screen; the mighty chorus is sung.

Yes, but living isn't a baseball game, and it is no more certain than the color, make, and model of police cars. Living *is* a sea of change, and everyone of us is caught up in it. There was a time when you could count on working for the same company for thirty or forty years, knowing that if you invested in the company, they would invest in you. That time is gone forever, and now people have to be flexible, knowing that their job and all that goes with it — self-esteem, security, the means of caring for your family — all of it can vanish in a moment. There was a time when school was the safest place in the world; that, too, is gone forever. Living in a society where there are far more guns than people, no place is entirely safe, neither schools nor the local McDonald's. It is our daily walk: life ... is fragile; it can change in an instant. A phone call from extended family in the middle of the night, the tough words you dread to hear from the physician, the surreal drama unfolding in your marriage when your life partner says, "No more; I'm leaving. I don't love you anymore; I'm not even sure if I ever did" — all this and more are the heart-ripping brutal reminders that little, if anything, is really certain other than uncertainty. Then, in the seventh inning of our lives, what song do we sing, what chorus do we hear? We know the answer to that: sometimes it's a quiet whimper, sometimes a loud wail. Its origin is the lived experience of our often ambiguous and more often senseless lives. From a confused mind or a broken heart it rises, given voice by our despair. We know the words; we know the haunting melody. Do we, on this day, know something else? Do we know a different song, another melody, this one proclaiming victory, this one sung to the tune of joy and hope?

God's Good News for our lives today is one, that there is such a song and melody; two, God is ready to teach it to us, to plant it in our heart; and three, there is a time to sing it, and it is not in the seventh inning of our lives, when it's almost over. So says the Seer in his fantastic vision of life and death and all that is between and beyond. Look with him with eyes of faith, and we, too, shall see and hear.

With highly symbolic language, John describes what truly transcends description. He sees a multitude, worshiping God, all joining in a song of victory. We know it's a song of victory, for they have shed their tattered rags and are clothed in new, white robes. They wave in their hands the palm branch of victory; and even the opening word of the chorus speaks of victory, for the word translated "salvation" can also be translated "victory." How can this be, given the fact that their puny lives have been crushed by the power of a demonic Emperor — for this is the "great tribulation" John has in mind: the very real tribulation of a persecuted church at the close of the first century — how can this be? It can be because they have discovered the truth about living! Victory and liberation belong to God, and it is in the power of God that we know victory! It is the truth Jesus flung in the face of his accusers as we read in the Gospel of John: "My Father," says Jesus, "is greater than all" (John 10:29), and all who are in Christ shall triumph over all that is destructive to living. All in Christ shall know and sing the song of victory! You see, there really is a song of victory; God has given it to us, Easter people, the Body of the Risen Christ. Sometimes neither the words nor the melody come easily; sometimes the words seem empty, the tune discordant. But this does not mean there isn't the song, nor does it mean we cannot sing it! First, of course, we have to learn it. Are you ready? Then let John teach us. Look at what gave the martyrs victory. It wasn't their death; that's too easy: we all die. No, it was their life that gained the victory, their life lived in faithful response to the victory God had already achieved. Allow me to unpack that for a moment.

God has already won the victory over all that is destructive to human living. The victory is not in doubt, but in the life, death, and resurrection of Jesus — the "Lamb who was slain," to use John's terminology — the victory is an accomplished fact. God has demonstrated who really is worthy of worship, and what power really is the strongest power. And it was not the Emperor, nor violence, nor brutality. Neither is it all that is around us competing and conflicting for our allegiance and worship. Rather, it is God and God alone who is worthy of worship, and it is self-giving love which is the triumphant power. You see, the "great tribulation" may have been a historical event, but the time of testing of God's people is timeless. Always and in every generation — including and especially this one — the people of God are in danger of being seduced by the Lie, by what is illusion and unworthy of our allegiance and worship. The name of the emperor just changes a bit: once it was Domition or Nero — now it's your bank account, or stock portfolio, or the things you've accumulated, or unrestrained self-centeredness. Given the victory of God, what response, then, shall we make to it? If we, like those who have gone before us are to be conquerors — and notice that this is another rendering of the word we translate "martyr"; the same word can be translated conqueror, or "victor," as well as "witness" — if we are to be victors, then the choice is obvious. We become conquerors when we trust and worship God! We stake our very lives on the victory of God in the liberating love of Christ, and in living that love and fidelity, we, too, shall sing the song of victory! This is what John is teaching us; it is how we learn the song. Yes, and we shall sing it now!

"Really?" you say. Can we really sing it now? Let's be honest with each other. Right now, it's hard for some of us to sing the song of victory. Right now, our lives are stressed and stretched. Right now, we don't feel all that victorious, all that joyful. We feel burdened and saddened by failure and heartaches. We feel the silence of not knowing love, or companionship, or hope. We feel the sadness of separation from the God who often seems distant and silent. Songs are hard right now; so we really wonder, "Can I really sing the song of victory now?" Maybe later, in a different time and place — but right now? Absolutely! We can absolutely sing it now! It doesn't matter if we're ten runs behind, we still can sing the song, for there is no better time than the present. Once again the Seer lets us see it. In his conversation with the Elder about who the chorus is, the Elder tells John, "These are those who are coming through the great tribulation" (Revelation 7:14), and they are still singing! You see, it's an ongoing, ever-present, ever-now reality! We are always in the midst of testing and stress; we are always coming through the great tribulation. It is an every day challenge.

This is why not only is there no better time than the present to sing the song of victory; there is no time other than now to sing! We're not going to see a time and moment when we are not in tribulation — at least not this side of living!

Get to your feet, then, Christians! The victory is won! Of this, we can be certain! It's time to sing! The music is playing; the words are on the screen; the chorus waits only for your voice and my voice to join in.

Easter 5

Creating Family

Revelation 21:1-6

The issue was one of survival. Under the Belknap Bridge Viaduct of "Cowtown" in the early 1930s small clapboard houses found their niche sandwiched among the railroad tracks. It was low income, rental housing that served both the workers on the Cotton Belt and Rock Island Lines (for Ft. Worth in those days was not only a cattle trading center; it was also a major railroad town) as well as providing homes for what we now call "the underclass."

One of those was a woman older than her 27 years, mother to four children, wife to a besotten woman chaser. In the late afternoon sun, walking home from work at the nearby factory, she did not see the switching mesh clearly, stumbled, and lodged her foot in the vortex of the tracks. It was the wrong time and place. She was no match for the oncoming locomotive, and she died at the scene. She didn't survive, but her children did, only because her younger sister, not yet married but on the threshold of engagement, took custody of the children, delayed her own marriage for almost ten years, rearing the children until the oldest could assume that responsibility. It was an act of self-giving, self-sacrificing love that created family where none really was.

Now, in your mind's eye, fast-forward the scene. It's still in Cowtown, but now the holding pens on the Northside are almost all gone, and Swift and Co. has already pulled out, with the Armour Packing operation soon to shut its doors. What remains, however, is the issue of survival. The woman who was "mom" to the four children in 1932 is now twenty years older, with two children of her own. It's 5 a.m., and she is struggling to get up, still weary from her moonlighting job selling beer and hot dogs at the Northside Arena, where bull riding was the main event. Knowing that five hours of sleep isn't enough for anyone, she also knows that the bus to her day job comes at 6 a.m., and she needs to be ready. There is a reason: the children need to eat; the rent needs to be paid. So she goes and comes, and this goes on for almost as long as anyone can remember until her two sons can start working themselves and their mother can give up the evening job, knowing that she did it; they survived as a family. How? Because of self-giving, self-sacrificing love; it created family and enabled it to survive.

It *is* a matter of survival. On this day, in this place we call home, and in homes throughout our nation, it is a matter of survival for families. In far too many homes the threat to authentic family *is* poverty and all the deprivation that goes with it — the lack of adequate nutrition, the environment of defeat and despair, sub-standard educational opportunities, the threat of violence, and the ever-present temptation of drugs as the means of escaping it all; these all create an issue of survival for families mired in poverty. But poverty and the war-zone neighborhoods it creates are not the only threat; survival of authentic family life transcends the poverty line; it is more complex than just poverty and environment. It has to do with work and wealth taking the place of time with each other, with schedules that never allow any time for sharing intimacy. It has to do with parents not parenting, with television being the babysitter, with books and music, museums and theater being unknown relics of the past. It has to do with the disappearance of faith being practiced in the home and reinforced in the community of faith. It has to do with all of this and more, and these are powerful forces ripping at the fabric of family life, forces which are calling into serious question the survival of family. And I do *not* mean family as some would focus on it; I mean family in all of its diversity: single parent families, mom and dad and two-children families, families where grandparents are the parents, once-married and never-married families, and all the rest. You know the threat to the survival of authentic family. You live with it constantly in your own family. You and I also know why meeting and overcoming the threats to family is so important. Survival of family life is not just so card companies and floral shops and restaurants can have a big day on Mother's Day. No, authentic family life is so important because it is where life is both created and nurtured. It's where self-esteem and personal worth are discovered. It is the place of support and love and growth. It is the arena where learning and faith happens and real values are inculcated. It is the place where we learn how to love with compassion and caring, and to survive in every sense of the word. We do not have to be sociologists or psychologists — even Christian psychologists! — to know this. We know it because we are living it; we are trying to survive it.

Today, Scripture is inviting us to know something else, something essential in our struggle to create family and ensure its survival. There is a way to do this, and Scripture can show us how. The way is immersed and wrapped up in this scene of cosmic survival, pictured for us by John the Elder. John says that he sees: he sees a time when all that is destructive to life will vanish, and in its place will be perfect wholeness and peace, a new heaven, a new earth. But John sees more than this. He sees the reason for a new heaven, a new earth, a time of healing and wholeness for the entire created order. The reason is the absolute victory of self-giving, self-sacrificing love. And seeing all of this, John knows that his vision is not just a vision of a "might be future," it is also a vision of a "can be present." As is the case in the entire structure of Revelation, so it is in today's text: John sees not only what shall be, growing out of what has been, but he especially sees what is. This is because John's understanding of time in the arena of God's action does not flow in a linear fashion of past, present, and future, but it is spiral, moving back and forth, up and down, all held together in one pregnant moment. And the moment comes when God comes in the presence of Christ's all victorious self-giving, self-sacrificing love.

Now we see it, don't we? The dwelling of God *is* with persons when love happens; when love happens, new heavens and a new earth are created; when love happens, healing and wholeness do come — and it is all an ever present possibility, because the end is not an event; it is a *person*! Do you remember the words of the One on the throne? — "I am making all things new, for *I* am the beginning and the end." That is to say, "I" (not an event). "*I* am the source of all life, all meaning in its never-ending possibility."

Hear with hope and joy the words from the One who sits on the throne! God's Good News for us today is that in our time and place, in our very real "now," God can be the source of new possibilities, the ending of fractured family, and the beginning of new, authentic family. As John says so powerfully, it happens as all new life and possibility happen: in self-giving, self-sacrificing love. Such love creates, re-creates, and marks us as a family, both in and out of the church. We know this in the truth of Jesus' own words which are repeated again and again in the Fourth Gospel, even as we read them in John 15:12, "Love one another, even as I have loved you," for it is by this love that a witness to the truth of God and the real possibilities of living in all relationships are made. So if you and I really want to make it happen here and now, and not in some distant, far-off future, this is how we do it: we, in our families, let loose the power that not only creates and recreates new heavens and a new earth, bringing healing and wholeness in the cosmic sense; we let loose the power of self-giving, self-sacrificing love that creates and re-creates the most important relationships God has given us, our relationships with those who are our family.

The answer we make to three questions holds the answer for us: The first one is, "Whose needs are being served by my choices and behavior?"; the second one is, "What expression of self-giving, self-sacrificing love really meets those needs?"; and the third one is, "How can I be an instrument of grace and reconciliation when the bond of love is fractured?" When we get the answers to these three questions right, family will be created!

It really begins with how we sort out and live out, "Whose needs are being served?" If you and I took that seriously in our families, think of the transformation we would see. The growth, nurture, and well-being of those with whom we share our lives would be the center of our action, not ourselves! It would re-create our life together! Of course, it is not always easy to know how to serve someone else's needs, and this is why we need the answer to the second question, "What expression of self-giving, self-sacrificing love really meets those needs?" You see, sometimes authentic love means making tough choices and setting limits; sometimes we really have to operate on the basis of needs, not "wants" — and they aren't always the same. So we really need to think about expressing authentic love and living that out, not just doing what is easy or expedient.

So it is that the truth of living is not only that self-giving, self-sacrificing love creates family; it is also the truth that sometimes, in spite of our love, families fracture, the bond of love fractures. What do we do then? Then, we try to answer the third question, "How can I be an instrument of grace and reconciliation in this relationship?" And you see where this is headed, don't you? It takes you back to the first question ("Whose needs are being served?), which then moves you to the second ("What expression of love will meet those needs?"), which — when it doesn't happen — moves you to the third one about being an instrument of grace when the bond is broken. It is all wrapped up together in one pregnant moment of self-giving, self-sacrificing love. This is how it happens; this is how family is created and constantly re-created: It happens when authentic, self-giving, self-sacrificing love happens.

Will it always happen? Will love always come alive and fracture become healed and family created and re-created? Sadly, the answer to that question is, "No, not always; at least not this side of our ultimate end in God." As the Seer says, only God's love and the victory in God's love are sure things; even the heavens and the earth shall pass away; only God's love remains. So the survival of any family is always up for grabs. But this is no reason to give up! If we give up, we know for certain what happens: nothing! Grab this, then, on a scale far smaller than John's cosmic vision, but intensely personal and absolutely critical: when the issue is survival — and it is, it really is — the world may be in God's hands, but our family is in ours. Given the truth of it, which will you choose: to *try* and fail — or, to *fail* at trying?

Easter 6

If You Hate To Wait, Try This

Revelation 21:10, 22—22:5

I am certain someone dreamed up the idea long before I encountered it in its tubular steel reality, but I like to think it started there, where I first saw it, in southern California, at Universal Studios, the land and place of illusion. Bars — not the places you go to socialize (we have those here!) — but steel bars, arranged so as to force large numbers of waiting people into serpentine columns. You see them everywhere now, even at your local fast-food restaurant. Some engineering genius might explain their function as "proper space utilization." That is to say, by means of them you can force large numbers of people into a very compact space, snaking them back and forth, back and forth — rather than in one long perpendicular line.

I don't think so; I don't think this is what they're about. I think they were created to seduce us through illusion. I think they were dreamed up, like any good movie, to make you think what you're looking at is real — when it isn't! What you see is a line that looks like its only ten feet long; but if you uncoiled it, it would be a hundred feet long. I think they do this so when you're waiting you don't realize you're waiting. Of course, if you stand there long enough, reality eventually sets in; you're no longer fooled; you know the thing is moving like ketchup out of a bottle.

You and I have been standing in place long enough; we are no longer fooled. We know we're waiting, and the wait has gone on far too long. Yes, we are waiting, and it isn't a movie; it isn't illusion; and we aren't fooled. It is like ketchup out of a bottle; it is way too slow! It is too slow for fractured families and fractured relationships to know healing; it is too long a wait for empty lives to be filled with some sense of hope, purpose, and joy. The time to come for alienation to be overcome — a time when distance between ages and races and all of the divisiveness in this land to be transcended, and a real sense of community to emerge — this time is way too long in coming. It is too slow for the celebration of diversity to come, for a love for other persons that rises above selfishness to come: too long and too slow for any and all of it to happen.

Stretched and challenged by what is — a world seemingly filled with hatred and brutality — we wait for what can be: a world healed of hurt, filled with peace. In our own world, our own private world in which each of us are living — whatever the hurt — as well as in the public world we can all see, we are waiting. And the longer we wait, the more anxious (maybe even cynical) we become. We wonder while we wait. Is there any point to it, to the waiting? Will anything be different; will we be different? Can I even dare to hope for peace and healing — in my own life, much more so for peace and healing to come to the world in which I live? And what about God? What about the caring, compassionate, interested-in-me-and-my-hurt God? Delayed, as well as deaf? Or maybe this "trust in God" thing is just like the shark in the lake, and the sponge boulders on the hill, and the *Psycho* house on the movie lot: it's just an illusion; not real at all; someone else's script, but not mine; God for them, maybe, but not for me. Don't you just hate it?

If you hate it, if you hate to wait, try this: "slow" doesn't mean "never"; "once then" *does* mean "now again." This is the one good reason — the only good reason — to wait at all. It is the one and only way to live with any sense of hope in this admittedly confusing present: it is because of what God did and is continuing to do — until nothing more will have to be done. This is what John saw in his vision of the New Jerusalem, and it is what he's inviting us to see. John looked and saw what was, what had happened. Part of it wasn't a pretty sight. He saw a world gone mad ("drunk" was the word he used) with its worship of violence and brutality. He saw a culture totally seduced by materialism and wealth, and the profound cheapening of the values of love and compassion and care for others. John saw the ridicule and persecution of God's faithful people, the disappearance of faith and hope, and the near-triumph of despair and cynicism. It was ugly. Yes, but he saw something else, too; he saw something of a radiant beauty. It wasn't the near-triumph of despair and cynicism, but it was the absolute triumph of God's victory of self-giving love in Jesus, the Christ. John saw that, in spite of how powerful evil and hatred, violence and brutality all were, God's love was more powerful! Jesus won the victory! In Jesus, God reached across the abyss of human alienation, bridged the gap, and came to persons with healing and renewal.

This is what John saw, and for him it was fact; it had already happened. So when he saw "what *would* be," it was really seeing *now again* what *once was*. This is why in his vision of the New Jerusalem coming down from God, John chooses so carefully his words: it is a continuous action! That is to say, the New Jerusalem is *always* coming down out of heaven from God, for God is always coming to persons, bringing healing and renewal; and God will keep on coming until all the created order is healed and made new, and God doesn't *have* to come anymore — for nothing accursed and undone will be left. Then, the Tree of Life will have done its job; its leaves will have healed the nations. The River of Life will have done its job: all the earth will be refreshed by the life-giving Spirit of God. And God in Christ will have done God's job: the perfection of creation at its beginning — before we messed it up — will have been restored. No wonder in John's language it is heaven!

But is it now? And if it isn't, how much longer are we going to have to wait? Let's be real with each other: we don't see any new Jerusalem, either here or coming; and it seems like we have been waiting a long long time. Well, yes! But also, "No!" — because the coming of God's healing, hope-giving presence — "heaven," if you will — is both "now" and "not yet." Such is God's word of hope, in the waiting, for us. God's "coming down" to persons with healing and renewing power (what John calls "heaven") *is* here, right now. But it is only here in part, not in completeness; that's later, and later *will* come. We can count on it, because of what God has already done and is continuing to do.

Do we hear it, the word of hope? Can we see it, the reason to hope? Try this. Look, and see a community of faith, where lives are transformed by the healing and renewing presence of God. You see, the community of faith is a sign that God is with us, that God continues to do what God has been doing. Lives *are* being changed. Alienation *is* being overcome. People *are* being affirmed as persons of ultimate value and worth; diversity *is* being celebrated; love *is* alive — and the church is a witness to it. It is real!

Listen, and hear the voice of the One who says, "It is for *you*!" God has bridged the abyss of your alienation, and has come to you; God is in this present moment offering healing of your broken heart and broken life; God is ready to renew you! Heaven is here and ready for you to step into it with joy and celebration. It *is* the word of hope!

Look and listen, see and hear that nothing and no one shall be beyond God's living re-creative reach. It is universal, even cosmic, in its scope. It is God's intention to heal and restore all of creation through the power of love, even those who oppose God and have made war on God's people. It is what God is about, and if this isn't heaven, what is?

Look and see, listen and hear; and then, when you and I have looked, seen, and heard enough, try this: in this present moment, in this present place, and in our present lives we are the ones who are God's instruments in bringing it all about: heaven, the place and time when persons are in the presence of God. You see, God's hands that bridge the gap of human alienation and hurt, the hands that bring the New Jerusalem, are *our* hands; it is the way God does things. Ours are the hands that heal and renew; ours are the hands of love that lift up the broken and bleeding of this world. Ours are the hands that reach out and include, that make a place in this place for all persons. Ours are the hands that touch a child, feed the hungry, clothe the naked. Ours — the hands of God.

So while you're waiting — and hating it — try this: bring hope to someone, embrace with love, be an instrument of grace, a part of heaven. In doing it, you and I will discover something, something really important for the living of these days: the more you share in the doing, the less it seems like waiting. That isn't illusion; it's fact.

Why Life Changes When You Know The Truth

Ephesians 1:15-23

If you live long enough, you will come to know the truth of it: "What goes around, comes around." Fifty years ago people waited in line near the old stadium in downtown Cleveland to get a World Series ticket and watch the Indians play. Thirty years ago they waited all night to get tickets to see and hear Mick Jagger, Keith Richards (every mother's dream date for her daughter), and the rest of the Stones. Twenty-two years ago it was to see the new film phenomenon created by George Lucas, *Star Wars*, with all of its digital creatures, an aging Alec Guiness, and a young Harrison Ford.

In 1999, George Lucas did it again. It came around again: another incredible journey into "a long time ago, in a galaxy far, far away" as we were swept along into galactic fantasy toward the *Phantom Menace*. There was a new plot, new heroes and villains, new creatures, but one thing was not-so-new: the unabashed and intentional spirituality embedded in the film. "What goes around, comes around," and *this* has come around again.

George Lucas knows something about this culture, and particularly about its "Gen-Xers" and "Millennials" that is worth us knowing. There is both a deep spiritual hunger, as well as a perceived spiritual vacuum, in this nation. It is not just the province of the younger generations, although it is perhaps most deeply felt there. There is a profound searching going on, but not a lot of finding.

George Lucas knows this, and he has intentionally made his film to probe this hunger and search. Interviewed by Bill Moyers in a national news magazine, Lucas said, "I put the Force into the movie in order to try to awaken a certain kind of spirituality in young people — more a belief in God than a belief in any particular religious system. I wanted to make it so that young people would begin to ask questions about the mystery" (*Time*; Vol. 153, No. 16; April 26, 1999; p. 92).

Not only George Lucas, but you and I, whatever our age, have also lived long enough to know the truth of it: the questions — about the mystery — are not just the questions of the searching young; they are the questions of each and everyone of us; they are *our* questions. "Is there a 'mystery' at all? Or, are we just an accident of evolutionary determinism?" "Is what we think an experience of the mind and spirit really that? Or, is it all just a by-product of a bunch of neurons firing off?" "And if there *is* a 'mystery,' can it be penetrated and known? And if we penetrate it and come to knowledge of it, will any of this really make any difference in our lived experience?"

These are the questions. They are *our* questions, just as they have always been humanity's questions ever since human beings got to the place where they could eat without being eaten, and had time to sit down and sift through whether or not their miserable lives *have* any meaning. And we're still at it. "What goes around, comes around." You and I are on the search, the search to elucidate the mystery, because if we do, if we can penetrate it to the point where at least part of it is no longer mystery, then we might, just might, be able to make some sense out of our lives. We might discover what's really the truth about life — and death — and what's between, and what's beyond. And then, if we make that discovery — about what is true — why, then, our life might, just might, change! We might, just might, discover what authentic living is really all about, and then, whatever spiritual hunger, life hunger, we have might, just might, be satisfied.

Let me — better, let Scripture — tell you the truth of it: living in the midst of competing claims for what gives life meaning and purpose, hope and joy, God has made a definitive statement. In Jesus we can see and know not only what God is like, but we can also know what we can be like. Now this is not to say that there are not competing claims, any more than it is to say that there is no truth about God in any other expression of religion. We need to be guarded by and aware of human arrogance that would suggest that any human being — even a Christian one — can know all there is to know about God, and what God has been, is, and will be doing.

No, what the Scriptures of our Christian faith proclaim is not that we Christians have a corner on the market of religious truth, nor that no truth can be found in other faith expressions; not at all. What Scripture proclaims is that the truth of what God has been, is, and will be doing in Jesus the Christ transcends all these completing claims.

Moreover, if we can penetrate what God has been, is, and will be doing in Jesus the Christ — if we can know this truth — then your life and my life will change. As Jesus is recorded saying in the Fourth Gospel, "the truth [big "T"] will make you free" (John 8:32). This isn't some banal political bromide. Rather, it holds the possibility of spiritual freedom, the freedom to be set free from the bondage of empty and inauthentic living, and thus know and experience life with all power and purpose.

Praise God, we *can* know it! The prayer we read in Ephesians, a prayer for us and for all of hurting humanity, has been fulfilled! Hear it again, and in hearing it, enter into its power for you: "I am praying," says the author, "that you will have an openness to God's truth — that you 'will have the eyes of your hearts enlightened' — and that you will know the hope to which God has called you" (Ephesians 1:18). The hope, what the author calls the "riches of God's glorious inheritance" is what God has been, is, and will be doing in Jesus the Christ. It is the plan, the "mystery" as he calls it previously in verses 9 and 10, to renew and redeem — set free! — the entire created order. It is God's plan to bring wholeness and healing to all human fracture, to heal both the cosmos and all humanity in Christ — and this includes us!

This is God's answer to our questions. This is God's definitive statement, and it is the truth. What God is doing is pulling us in Christ toward the place and time when love triumphs, where broken hearts are healed and broken lives are made whole, where and when all bondage ceases, and we are set spiritually free to be all that God has intended us to be. It is the truth, both now and yet to be completed. This is what God has been, and is doing, and will continue to do until all creation is made whole in Christ, this galaxy and every other one.

If this is the truth (and it is; it really is), that our lives are being made whole and complete in Christ, when we buy into this truth and make it our living, our lives will change. Here is why; I want to lift up four reasons. First, your life will change because no more will you lie awake at night, or get up in the morning, wondering whether or not life has any meaning or purpose to it. You won't do that because the Truth says, "Life *is* going somewhere; all of human life, all that *is* is going somewhere!" There is purpose because God has a purpose for all of the created order — and that includes you and me, and everyone and everything else. We do not have to live lives empty of meaning, or filled with boredom. We do not have to try desperately to impose meaning on our days, or get so much "stuff" it doesn't matter. God's ultimate purpose has liberated us from cynicism, despair, and nihilism! God's purposes are at work, and God's purposes are heading somewhere. Knowing this will change your life!

The second reason why your life will change when you know the truth is this: Not only does God have a purpose for the creation, but God has also chosen to include you in God's work of renewal, healing, and wholeness. *You* count; all persons count ultimately to God. When you and I know this, our lives change. No longer do we live in bondage to our failure, our brokenness; no more do we think that we're just refuse, unworthy of love. The truth sets us free! The truth frees us to live lives of hope and joy, because when we know how much God loves us — enough to work within us toward completion and wholeness in Christ — how can we not leave all of our hurt and failure behind, stepping into God's new and glorious future?

The third reason life changes when we know the truth is wrapped up in how Jesus the Christ reveals God's purposes. That is to say, Jesus shows us where this thing is going; Jesus shows us what fulfilled human life can be like. So if you and I are wondering what this work is that God is doing in and with us — look to Jesus! There we can see what our lives can and will look like when God's purposes are unfolding. It can be a life of closeness with God. It can be a life lived in community with others. It can be a life filled with love and with all the joy love brings, and it can and will be a life lived ultimately with God.

The last reason why knowing the truth will change your life may be the most important of all. It is this: God is going to win! The truth says, "The victory is won!" When God raised Jesus from the dead and proclaimed that "Jesus is Lord!" — not violence, not brutality, not hatred, nor any other force or power we rightly call "demonic," but *Jesus* is Lord — when God acted definitively in Jesus the Christ, the victory was won. Oh, yes, there are times it may look in doubt. You can slow down God's purpose and side-track what God is doing, but you cannot stop it; you cannot defeat God. God is going to win! And you and I, we're going to make it! We are all going to make it; this beat up and battered world is going to make it, because in the end, God wins! Think how this changes everything! The truth liberates us from fear, despair, and anxiety. It fills our efforts with ultimate value. The truth gives us a new perspective — on life and death, and everything between and beyond — because, you see, it is all in God's hands. It *is* the truth, and it *will* set us free, free from all fear and hopelessness, both in this age and whatever age there is to come.

If we live long enough, we'll see it; we will come to know the truth: "What goes around, comes around" — and it is coming. If you and I are going to stand in line to see something, stand in line to see this.

Easter 7

God's Gift For Impatient People

Revelation 22:12-14, 16-17, 20-21

On the rare occasions when they would choose a direct confrontation, rather than their traditional hide-and-seek-ambush-then-melt-into-the-jungle guerrilla warfare at which the Vietcong were so adept, the conflagration would begin suddenly, two or three hours before dawn. This time was no exception. Their confidence bolstered by superior numbers, they had flanked the Marine fire-base on two sides and chose a direct assault through the wire around the perimeter. The din was incredible: rapid pops from automatic weapons' fire, the "woosh" then shattering explosions of mortars swept over them all. It was total chaos, a chaos vividly, frighteningly portrayed for those who have never experienced the terror and chaos of combat in the film *Apocalypse Now*. The anti-personnel mines that had been strung on the wire around the base served only to blow big, gaping holes in the perimeter, making the Marines all the more vulnerable. Then, with the whole surrealistic scene bathed in the erie glow of magnesium flares, he saw his buddy lying wounded, twenty, maybe thirty yards away. Without hesitation, or even really thinking, he left the wallow (foxhole is too glamorous a word) which afforded him some protection, crawled, scurried, zig-zagged to his friend, cradling him in his arms. Above the din and chaos of it all, he heard the words, "I knew you would come; I always knew you would come."

Do we? We are just shy of three decades from the wake-up call that was the Tet Offensive, and we are thousands of miles away from Vietnam. For those of us who lived through that horror, who saw the obscene waste of human life, who saw the fabric of this nation ripped asunder, and still carry within us the disillusionment and cynicism that was the bitter fruit of that conflict, for us, it seems light years away, bathed in its own surreal light of *Easy Rider* flickering before our eyes, overwhelmed by the din of Cream, Iron Butterfly, and all the rest.

The jungle, the fire fight, the chaos, the three-hour-pitch-darkness before the dawn remains, however; it all remains. The place and time have changed; the rest is the same. And lying wounded of heart and spirit, with hope and life ebbing, we wonder, "Will he come? Will *anyone* come?"

Get in touch with yourself for a moment: Where is your battlefield, your firefight, your jungle? Where is your darkness? Is it the darkness of failure, that confrontation with yourself in the dark night of your soul when you are forced to look at yourself, your life as it all really is — with all the hurt and pain you've caused yourself and others around you? Maybe your struggle is just trying to make it through one more miserable, empty, boring day — the struggle to sense some direction, some purpose for your life, the struggle to find some joy where you've known only heartache. Maybe the firefight you know is the combat with forces over which you have little or no control: illness that threatens your life; the death of a loved one; the illness or death of a relationship.

Whatever the nightmare is for you — or for me — none of us want it to continue; each of us longs for it to end. And the longer it continues, the more joy and hope drain away, the more fragile our faith in a loving, caring, ever-present God becomes. We grow increasingly impatient; we ache for something else. And in our struggle, in our longing, we live the truth of it: faced with what *is*, but wanting *what can be*, challenges faith, breeding both cynicism and despair.

In our impatience, God has both a gift and a promise for us. They are the gift and promise that can bring us peace and hope in the "now" as we wait for the "not yet." The gift is Christ who has come; the promise is that Christ will come. Such is the witness from Scripture for us today in John's epilogue to the vision God gave him. Remember how the revelation of John's vision began, even in the first verse of the first chapter. There the Seer says that the vision God has given him is a vision of "what must soon take place." That was almost 2,000 years ago! Was he wrong? Not at all! He was absolutely right! It *did* take place! But more to the point for us, it is *still* taking place, and it *will* take place — again and again — until God's work to bring all of the created order to its ultimate completion in Christ has taken place.

To understand this, and to understand its power for us, we need to again grasp John's understanding of time, time in God's arena of action. It is not "sequential." It is not "past, present, and future," but time in God's arena of action is concentric and spiral. What I mean by that is that past, present, and future move back and forth, up and down, all intertwined together. This is why "what must soon take place" not only *has*, but *is* taking place, *will* take place, again and again.

You see, Jesus is always coming to us, bringing his "recompense" (read, "reward"). Jesus is always coming to give us entry into the presence of God — which is his reward; Jesus is always coming to be the bright and morning star, to lift the darkness from our lives and to renew our battered hope. So above the din and in the darkness, in the chaos of our lives, when you and I are left on the battlefield of our own fire fight, with life and hope ebbing away, when we hear the Risen One say, "Surely I am coming soon," our response is that which has always been the response of the people of God: "Amen! Come, Lord Jesus!" Then, cradled in his arms, we shall be the ones to say, "I knew you would come; I always knew you would come."

How can this be? It's really quite simple; it requires no special revelation, no vision beyond that of seeing the person sitting next to you. We begin to understand it and see it all when we get the story straight: Jesus came to reveal the nature of God to us; he did that — or, as John says in his Gospel, he made known the "name" of God (John 17:26). That "name" is "self-giving, life-giving love"; in that love, Jesus created a community of persons — persons who are in Jesus, and because they are in Jesus they are in each other. Moreover, because Jesus is in them — "with" them — *now*, they shall always be with Jesus, and Jesus will always be with them. This is the story.

When you and I get the story straight, our eyes are opened, and we see it; that is, we see each other. We are this community Jesus has created; we are the people in Jesus and Jesus in us. So — now listen carefully! — when we come to each other, *Jesus* comes. Certainly this is not the only way Jesus comes, for Jesus comes in the Spirit, Jesus comes in the Sacraments, Jesus comes as we worship together in community, and so on. But this — "coming to each other" — is the most visible way Jesus comes.

You and I now begin to see it, don't we? *We* are God's gift to impatient people — all the people out there and in here who are lying there wounded by living, impatiently waiting for Jesus to come and heal them. *We* are God's gift to the broken-hearted and beaten down. We are God's gift to the hopeless and desperate, to the bored and cynical, to the poor and oppressed. We are God's gift to each and every one who, in the darkness and chaos of their lives, are waiting impatiently for Jesus to come, come and lift up, come and cradle in arms of love, come making new, giving hope, bringing the very presence of God. *We* are the gift! For in and through us, Jesus comes, comes to love and give life, comes to do it now.

I know and hear a lot of people — and I think you know them and hear them, too — who spend a lot of time talking about when Jesus is going to come back. I confess to you that I'm not very interested in Jesus coming back; I don't think John was either. Scripture is of one mind that God and only God knows when God will bring the created order to its completion, and we are constantly admonished in Scripture to give up silly speculation on this and quit wasting our time worrying about when Jesus is going to come back.

So I'm not very interested in Jesus coming back; but I am extremely interested in Jesus coming period! I am extremely interested in Jesus coming to the broken and hurting around us to bring healing and wholeness. I am very interested in Jesus coming to our youth and telling them they are loved; I am very interested in Jesus coming to the bored and hopeless, to men and women who are empty inside. I am interested in Jesus coming to the people around us in this community and city, to people who desperately need what Jesus can do in their lives. I am interested in Jesus coming to his

Church, overcoming its apathy and inertia, filling it with a passion to be a servant people; I *am* interested in Jesus coming period!

Maybe it's because I've been out there, broken and bleeding, in the darkness, with life and hope ebbing away, waiting, waiting ever so impatiently for Jesus to come and cradle me in his arms. Let me tell you, I am not alone! The battlefield is filled with the hurting, the hopeless; they, impatiently, are waiting; they are waiting for Jesus — which means they are waiting for us! They are waiting for you — and me — to give them that chance to say, "I knew you would come; I always knew you would come."

Books In This Cycle C Series

GOSPEL SET

Praying For A Whole New World
Sermons For Advent/Christmas/Epiphany
William G. Carter

Living Vertically
Sermons For Lent/Easter
John N. Brittain

Changing A Paradigm — Or Two
Sermons For Sundays After Pentecost (First Third)
Glenn E. Ludwig

Topsy-Turvy: Living In The Biblical World
Sermons For Sundays After Pentecost (Middle Third)
Thomas A. Renquist

Ten Hits, One Run, Nine Errors
Sermons For Sundays After Pentecost (Last Third)
John E. Berger

FIRST LESSON SET

The Presence In The Promise
Sermons For Advent/Christmas/Epiphany
Harry N. Huxhold

Deformed, Disfigured, And Despised
Sermons For Lent/Easter
Carlyle Fielding Stewart III

Two Kings And Three Prophets For Less Than A Quarter
Sermons For Sundays After Pentecost (First Third)
Robert Leslie Holmes

What If What They Say Is True?
Sermons For Sundays After Pentecost (Middle Third)
John W. Wurster

A Word That Sets Free
Sermons For Sundays After Pentecost (Last Third)
Mark Ellingsen

SECOND LESSON SET

You Have Mail From God!
Sermons For Advent/Christmas/Epiphany
Harold C. Warlick, Jr.

Hope For The Weary Heart
Sermons For Lent/Easter
Henry F. Woodruff

A Hope That Does Not Disappoint
Sermons For Sundays After Pentecost (First Third)
Billy D. Strayhorn

Big Lessons From Little-Known Letters
Sermons For Sundays After Pentecost (Middle Third)
Kirk W. Webster

Don't Forget This!
Robert R. Kopp
Sermons For Sundays After Pentecost (Last Third)